MARKETING SUPERPOWERS

Build a brand so good that getting
customers feels like magic

JON DAVIDS

Disclaimer

The information provided in this book is for general informational purposes only. The author and publisher make no representations or warranties of any kind, express or implied, about the completeness, accuracy, reliability, suitability, or availability of the information contained within these pages. Any reliance you place on such information is strictly at your own risk.

The author and publisher disclaim any liability for any loss or damage, including without limitation, indirect or consequential loss or damage, or any loss or damage whatsoever arising from the use of, or reliance on, the information presented in this book.

It is advised to consult with a professional for specific advice tailored to your situation. The author and publisher are not responsible for any actions or decisions made based on the information contained in this book.

ISBN: 978-1-7383152-0-8

What People Have Said About This Book

Jon breaks down complex marketing strategies into simple, practical steps that anyone can follow. If you want to grasp how marketing works today, this book is a must-read!

Lloyed Lobo | WSJ Best-Selling Author and Co-founder, Boast AI

Jon truly understands modern consumer behaviour and how word travels today. I've seen him develop these skills over the years, always staying on the pulse of culture. This book offers valuable insights to anyone building a business right now.

Joseph Mimran | Founder of Club Monaco, Joe Fresh, JM & Associates

Jon is a brilliant marketer who understands the landscape end to end and explains things in a way anybody can understand, digest and implement.

Bill Munro | Director at Munro Footwear Group

We already know marketers are superheroes, and books like this give us our superpowers. It is an essential read for anyone who wants to keep up in this fast-paced marketing world. And no one is more versed in the art and science of influencing than Jon Davids.

Brooke Janousek | CMO

Understanding the value of a brand, its ability to transcend consumer behavior — and building one that actually drives proÚit — is something so many entrepreneurs struggle with. Jon lays out a simple formula that's worked for ages, and still does.

Drew Green | Chairman, CEO and President, INDOCHINO

Jon's approach to explaining marketing and business strategies is simple, practical and most importantly, easy to understand and apply. He makes learning marketing fun and enjoyable.

Luis Velasco | SVP, Marketing Head at Jollibee Foods, North America

DEDICATION

To Alana — for always giving me time and space to do my creative writing.

To my mom — who when she heard I was writing a book, immediately asked if she could be the editor.

Thank you both for the endless support.

TABLE OF CONTENTS

Freebies from the Author

Hey, it's Jon Davids –

I'm so glad you've picked up a copy of my book. I hope the information inside transforms your abilities like it did for me.

To help you get the most out of it, I've created a bunch of worksheets, guides, and videos absolutely free.

You can grab them now at
JonDavids.com/MarketingSuperpowers

Or snap this QR code:

I share my insights every day across social media. You can follow me on all these platforms:

in linkedin.com/in/jondavids

▶ youtube.com/@jondavids

◯ instagram.com/jon_davids

𝕏 x.com/realjondavids

♪ tiktok.com/@realjondavids

And tune into my podcast every week. You can find it now at **JonDavids.com/Podcast**

Or snap this QR code:

BRAND

noun

Pronunciation: /brand/

Definition:

A brand represents every dollar your customer is willing to pay above and beyond what your product is worth.

So what's the upper limit of a brand?

Limitless.

Let's Begin: Why I wrote this book

I sucked at school. And that's not me being humble. Trying to sound like the everyman. I was just plain bad.

Not a bad kid. I just didn't get good grades. I was decent at some subjects. But mostly squeezed by on C'd and D's.

When I got to college, I had to take an elective course outside my major. So I went with a course called Intro to Marketing. Mostly because the timeslot fit nicely into my schedule.

And then something weird happened. I got a B.

At first it was hard to believe. Was this a mistake? Maybe I got someone else's transcript?

Nope. It was mine. I was officially a "B" student. In marketing. A subject I knew nothing about.

But I started to think about it more. I actually did kind of understand it. In its most basic form, marketing teaches you how to get people to buy stuff. Whatever it is you're selling. And because I was always entrepreneurial – working on my teenage side hustles – I found myself putting the lessons to work in real time.

Brand positioning, environmental analysis, the product matrix. It was academic, but it made sense to me.

It was then that it finally hit me. I wasn't a bad student. I was just never properly motivated.

Science, math, history… I couldn't care less. But now I was learning something useful. A system that gets people to give me their cash in exchange for my stuff. Now I was motivated.

Marketing became my obsession. And then it became my superpower. I was more than motivated. I was transformed.

Here's why.

We live in a world where people are too reasonable with their expectations. And that leads to limited thinking. They think growth is limited. They think money is limited. Their opportunity is limited. And their results are limited.

I have no interest in limited thinking. I have no interest in being reasonable. My expectations are unreasonable. And so are my results.

In this book you'll learn how I made $300,000 while I was still in college. You'll learn how I turned a YouTube channel into a cash-gushing business. You'll learn how I've used social media to drive millions in revenue for my marketing agency, Influicity.

And you'll learn exactly how to do it for yourself.

When marketing becomes your superpower, the limits melt away.

Growth is infinite. Money is abundant. Opportunities are everywhere. And they're calling your name.

As you get into marketing at an elite level, you'll understand psychology, motivation, instinct, reflex, perception, influence, pattern-matching, community, aspiration, value, and more.

Everything that makes the human mind function in a commercial transaction.

I'm going to get into all of these details throughout this book. I'm going to explain concepts that took me years to understand. I'll make it simple and practical.

Finally, I'll do for you what I wish someone did for me decades ago. I'll give you a crystal clear motivation.

Marketing is about providing endless amounts of value in exchange for endless amounts of money.

Money for your business, your shareholders, your employees, your family, your town, your economy, and your causes. And of course, for yourself.

Marketing is about making your message so good people are delighted to hand you their hard earned cash.

That's the motivation.

If you own a business or do marketing professionally — or if you hope to do either of those things one day — I wrote this book for you.

I love sharing these lessons because I know how life changing they can be. If you feel the same way, I encourage you to share this book with someone too. Give them this copy when you're done. Or if you don't want to wait, buy them a copy as a gift.

They say if you know how to sell, you'll never go hungry. I agree.

But I'll give you one better.

If you know how to market, you'll feed yourself and everyone around you, forever. And you'll still have leftovers.

That's why marketing is a superpower.

MARKETING SUPERPOWERS

Part 1

Introduction: How I learned the power of influence

I met a girl on YouTube. Then I sent her a message. She said yes. And it changed my life forever.

But no, it's not what you're thinking.

This is the story of how I learned about marketing superpowers. And it's important that I tell you how I learned it, so that you can appreciate how much of a game changer this was for me and my business. And how it could do the same for you.

When I say *marketing superpower*, I'm not talking about making a really good ad. Or coming up with a viral video idea. It's not some transactional marketing technique that will get you customers today and fade tomorrow.

I'm talking about building a growth machine so powerful that it gives you an inconceivably unfair advantage. Wildly unbalanced. So that when others look at how you trigger business growth, it seems like magic. Like watching Michael Jordan in the 1988 Slam Dunk Contest.

It's not magic. Believe me. No tricks and no illusions. Just a battle-tested playbook that works every single time.

I'm going to teach exactly how to do that in this book. And it starts with this story.

——

Rewind to 2011. I'm a young entrepreneur. Working on a really bad idea for an app. (I won't bore you with the app idea. But trust me, it sucked.)

During my research, I stumble across a 20-something woman making videos on YouTube. She's a video blogger. A "vlogger". Her name is Teresa.

I notice she's making videos daily. Mostly fashion hauls. That's where you go to Nordstrom or CVS and buy a bunch of stuff. Then turn on the camera and empty your bag so viewers can see what you bought.

Her videos are getting tons of views. Easily 30,000 a pop.

I'm confused. Who is this girl? Is she famous? How is she racking up these eyeballs? So I send her a message.

"Hey! I'm Jon. Quick question for ya – how are you getting all these views on your videos?"

Two hours later, Teresa responds. She tells me that she just makes them for fun, uploads them to YouTube, and people watch.

This is getting weird. But now I need to know more. I start typing.

"So it's all for fun, huh? And thousands of people are watching these videos where you talk about these products you're buying? Are any of the companies behind these products sponsoring you?"

"Nope," she replies.

This is wild. She's reaching 150,000 people a week, promoting huge makeup brands, and getting paid nothing. It's bending my brain.

I keep typing.

I tell her I just sold a digital advertising company. And I think she could be getting paid for these videos. A lot. Plus she would reach more people. Then I shoot my shot.

"I want to fly you in, put you up in a hotel, and have you make a video just like the ones you're making now. But this time, you'll do it for a brand. Featuring lots of products from one company. You game?"

"Sure!" she replies.

That was easy. Time to hustle.

I pull a few strings and convince a cosmetics company to let us film a video at their store. They definitely don't know what a "YouTuber" is. But this internet thing is exciting. So they agree.

Two weeks later, Teresa is in the store filming random beauty stuff. Next she posts it on YouTube.

And then it happens. She gets 54,000 views in 24 hours.

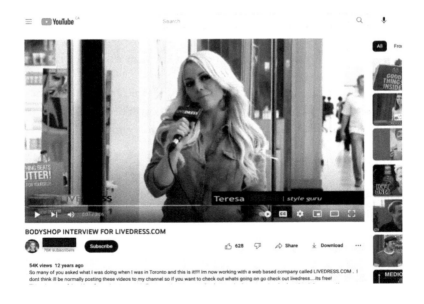

I can't believe this. It worked! I just discovered a marketing channel with loads of attention that is completely untapped by advertisers. As a business builder, this is gold.

The most difficult part of building and growing a company is getting customers. Lots of customers. And here was a channel that could bring in customers by the boatload.

I had seen the light. No looking back now.

———

Teresa was just a single YouTuber making videos on a single topic. But the opportunity here was huge. There were probably tons of people like Teresa. Making videos on every conceivable subject. Cooking, farming, travel, cars, tech, gaming, hunting, parenting, gardening, and more. If there weren't already, there would be soon. I could see it so clearly.

Teresa and I went on to work with loads of brands. I brokered the deals, she made the videos and we split the cash.

Eventually, this led me to build Influicity, so I could help way more companies on a much higher level.

We started by just focusing on influencer marketing. My first 3 clients were a movie studio, a makeup brand, and a car company. We built a name and a reputation as the go-to influencer marketing agency. Back when that wasn't even a thing.

Then we began to make podcasts for brands, run their social media channels, manage their paid advertising, get them higher in search results, and a lot more. Through working with mid-size businesses all the way up to Fortune 500, we've learned how influence travels through culture. From a crowded urban center to a quiet rural town. How word spreads among 14-year old girls, 42-year-old executives, soccer moms, jet setters, bookworms, foodies, fashionistas, tech bros, empty nesters, and beyond.

And most importantly, we help our clients build communities around their brands. In the same way Teresa did it on YouTube. Because every brand needs to do this. Or get left behind. Relegated to irrelevance.

I want to emphasize how transformative the Teresa story was. All the work we did together, all the products we sold, all the brands we served – everything was because of influence.

Call it audience, community, fan base, followers, or advocates. There's a big vocabulary when it comes to this stuff. But I don't like using big words. I'm keeping it simple so you can understand everything I'm saying and get the most out of it.

This book is my effort to tell you everything I know about how to build a community for your brand, nurture that community, scale that community, and provide them tons of value.

Do all this, and I promise, your marketing will feel like magic.

SECTION 1

The Axis of Influence

CHAPTER 1

Busting Myths

Let's get one thing straight. Getting popular is not complicated. It follows a simple path. The path is not straight, nor is it predictable. And it's definitely not easy.

But it is simple.

I know this because I've been around influencers for many years. More than a decade. I've studied thousands. And I've done it all for myself.

Understanding how influential people carve their path makes total sense. In retrospect. Which means we can reverse-engineer it.

Once you learn how to do it and put these steps into action, the results are ludicrous. You feel like Mario jumping on the mushroom. Everything is just a bit easier.

People assume that getting popular is a matter of luck. And while there is some luck involved in the velocity and timing of your influence, a lot of it can be architected. You just need to understand the mechanics of becoming popular.

Whether it's a person, a brand, or a combination of both, there's a deviously simple road that will move something from complete anonymity to household name.

And I can explain it all to you right now, with the *Axis of Influence*.

CHAPTER 2

Welcome to the Axis of Influence

The Axis of Influence is my visual explanation of precisely how anyone or anything gets popular.

Within the Axis of Influence there are 2 factors:

1. How much reach you have. This is the "Y axis".

2. How known, liked, and trusted you are. For short, I'll refer to this as *KLT*. This is the "X axis".

You can see a visual of this in Diagram 1.

We need to understand both the Y and X axis for the next part to make sense. So let's look at each one now.

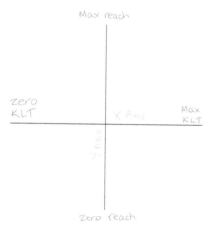

Diagram 1: The Axis of Influence. Notice the Y axis and X axis.

Reach: the Y Axis

At the very bottom of the Y Axis is "zero reach". And at the very top is "maximum reach".

Think of *reach* as how loud your voice is. To explain this, I'll use a character named Jake.

Jake is sitting in a room by himself. He has zero reach. He can certainly speak, but no one will hear him. Even if Jake yells, he remains silent as far as anyone else is concerned. He's isolated and alone.

Now let's say Jake wanders out of his little room and finds a group of 10 people mingling in the lobby. He asks for their attention and starts to speak. These 10 people are all within earshot of Jake. So when Jake speaks, all 10 people can hear him.

He's not saying anything different. It's the same stuff as before. His words hold the same meaning, but they have a bit more value now because 10 people are around to listen. They may or may not be interested, but at least he has the opportunity to grab their attention.

Jake keeps walking and opens the door to an auditorium. He steps up onto a stage and grabs the microphone. Out in the audience, there's a crowd of 100 people. He starts to speak. Again, he's saying the same things as before. But now his words are carrying even more value because there are 100 people listening. Just like in the lobby, some people are really interested and others aren't. But at least they can all hear him.

Now a red light flickers on. It's a camera and it's pointed straight at Jake. He's being live streamed on YouTube. And 10,000 people are tuning in. His mouth opens and the same words come out. He's repeating what he said in his little room by himself, in the lobby to 10 people, and on the stage to 100 people.

His reach is growing because more people are hearing him when he speaks.

But keep in mind, these people don't necessarily know who Jake is. He's able to reach them because of the mechanisms at his disposal. First the lobby, then the stage, and then the livestream. Reach grows simply because you can connect with more people at one time.

But do these people care what Jake says? Are they seeking him out? Will they remember him tomorrow?

Not necessarily. Having reach is just half of the Axis.

Think about it. Jake could just be the dude calling out the letters at a BINGO tournament. Everyone hears him, but do they know his name? Are they going to stand in line to meet him? Or buy a product because he recommends it?

Nope.

Jake is reaching people, but reach alone is not influence. You also need KLT. The two work hand in hand.

For now, you know what reach is. So let's look at the X Axis.

Known, Liked, and Trusted: the X Axis

For someone to be influential, they must be known, liked, and trusted. We call this KLT.

At the far left side of the X axis is zero KLT. And at the far right side is maximum KLT.

Being *known* is when you have some recognition in other peoples' minds. They know your name, or your face, or your logo, or your symbol. Or something that represents who you are. That's the starting point.

Being *liked* is when those same people who know you, have an affinity towards you. They relate to you. They derive value from you. They associate good things with you. And they feel good when you enter their mind.

Being *trusted* is when those same people who know and like you, truly value what you say. They seek out your recommendations, feedback, advice, commentary, validation, strategies and insights. They put weight in your words. They might even buy a product purely because your name is on it.

Put these ingredients together, along with reach, and now you actually have influence.

Obviously, there are different degrees to all these things. A gal on TikTok might be known. And the President of the United States is also known. But one is clearly *more known* than the other.

Similarly, you could like a novel you just read. And you could like your favorite rock band. But you might like one more strongly than the other.

And when it comes to trust, it's one thing to trust a tech guy on YouTube and another to trust a surgeon who's about to perform a medical procedure. It's a different degree of trust.

Generally, the more intense your KLT, the higher your level of influence.

It's also important to cover the opposite side of KLT. I'll call it anti-KLT. I'm going to get into this more in Section 6, but here's a brief overview.

Everyone has haters. Critics. Nay-sayers. Frenemies. And as you gain more KLT, the anti-KLT gets louder.

Anti-KLT is when people know you, but they don't like you, they definitely don't trust you, and they want everyone to know that. They scream it from the rooftop, evangelizing how outrageous your thoughts are and how people would have to be nuts to take you seriously.

Thank goodness for these people. You're going to need them. But again, I'll get to that later.

Now you understand reach and KLT. So let's zoom out to the full Axis of Influence.

CHAPTER 3

Understanding the Axis

The Axis has 4 quadrants: Top left, top right, bottom left, bottom right.

We'll start at the bottom left quadrant.

Bottom left: Anonymity

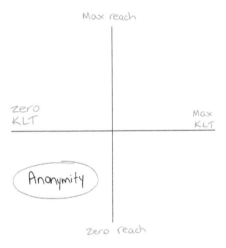

Diagram 2: The bottom left quadrant on the Axis of Influence. This is called Anonymity.

The bottom left quadrant is called *Anonymity*. You can see this in Diagram 2. It's a sad name and a sad place to be if your goal is influence. But cheer up my friend – everyone starts here.

Well, almost everyone. If you happen to be born into a famous family, then you might never be anonymous. Similarly, if a mega-company launches a new brand, they might have a hard time keeping a low profile.

But these are edge cases and the playbook is similar either way. So let's assume that your brand – like 99% of the planet – is starting from anonymity.

When you're in the bottom left, you have zero reach and zero KLT. In other words, you're a total unknown. Get comfortable, because you're going to be here for a while. And that's a good thing.

You'll use this time in anonymity to sharpen your skills. When you're an unknown, you have the luxury of messing up in the dark.

We make mistakes in the shadows so we can shine in the sunlight. No judgment, no prying eyes. And that's a serious luxury.

Top Right: Mass Influence

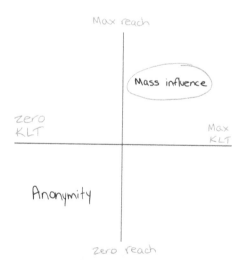

Diagram 3: The top right quadrant on the Axis of Influence. This is called Mass Influence.

Let's move our attention to the top right quadrant, as you'll see in Diagram 3. This quadrant is called *Mass Influence*. Here we'll find the most well-known, liked, and trusted icons in the world.

Think Coca-Cola, Oprah Winfrey, Google, Taylor Swift, and The Pope. These people and brands are at the peak of reach and KLT.

When they make a move or utter a word, the world listens. They create echoes. Gossip. Headlines. Water cooler talk. Taylor Swift can say something on X and it will be re-posted to multiple platforms, hundreds of times a minute for hours to come. It will trend on social media. It will be picked up by news channels and podcasts. It will be dinner table conversation. Forwarded in emails. Praised and ridiculed. Analyzed like crazy. Just a few simple words posted online by someone who sits in Mass Influence will reverberate endlessly.

Cool. So how can we get there?

Slow down – I'm not even sure you should be there yet. We'll get to that.

First we need to look at the 2 other quadrants.

Top left: 15 Minutes of Fame

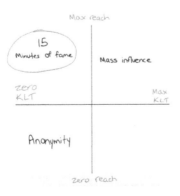

Diagram 4: The top left quadrant on the Axis of Influence. This is called 15 Minutes of Fame.

Let's look at the top left quadrant, as you'll see in Diagram 4. I call this *15 Minutes of Fame*. And you should try to avoid this at all costs.

You see, it's so tempting to rapidly climb the Y Axis, gaining reach as fast as you can. But there's a big problem. Without any KLT, you'll come crashing down just as fast. We see this happen all the time.

Songs that saturate the airwaves, only to be forgotten 2 weeks later. Social media trends that catch fire. Then fizzle out. New restaurants that are so popular you can't get a table. Then they're out of business. (And you still can't get a table).

Reach gives you altitude. It makes your megaphone bigger. But KLT is your fuel. You need it to keep going. For the public to maintain their interest.

There are some cases where a brand seemingly comes out of nowhere and rockets up in popularity. And then they manage to hold their reach and relevance. But from all the cases I've seen, this isn't the reality.

These brands didn't appear out of nowhere. They've been around for a long time. Building KLT in the shadows. Nurturing their base of core fans.

Maybe you just heard of them 8 minutes ago, but that doesn't mean they're new.

These brands have been growing KLT for a long time. It just took a little longer for you to notice.

You should stay away from chasing a fleeting 15 minutes of fame. You need to build and nurture a community. And that takes some time.

Bottom Right: Niche Influence

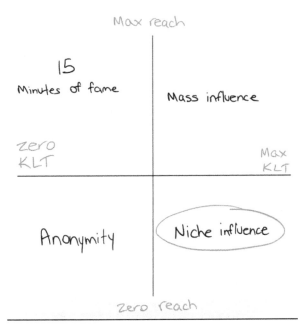

Diagram 5: The bottom right quadrant on the Axis of Influence. This is called Niche Influence.

We've arrived in my favorite place of all. It's called Niche Influence, which you'll see in Diagram 5.

Breathe it in my friends. We have now entered the coveted territory where so much brand wealth is built. Pay close attention here. Because there's riches in these niches.

Niche influence is where 95% of successful brands live. They build a tribe, plant their flag, and dominate their category. In fact, many of the biggest companies in the world have niche influence. And this becomes more true every day, as attention splinters and consumers build their own brand bubbles.

Think about the software you use at work. Or your favorite dessert. Or that show you've been streaming. Or the app on your phone that you click into 7 times a day. Or that new band your friend just told you about. Or that book you can't put down.

If you walked up to a stranger on the street and mentioned any one of these things, would they know what you're talking about? Do you think those brands would mean as much to them as they do to you?

Probably not.

And that's a good thing. It means these brands have tapped into a hugely valuable market and asserted their dominance. Owning a niche can be enormous. It means you have loads of KLT and scalable reach. You don't reach everyone, just the people who really matter.

The consumer's optionality is endless right now. We live in a swipe and click culture. That means we can all dial in our preferences and find a product, person, or brand that's an exact match for what we want.

So as a business, when you find yourself in Niche Influence, you are doing very well. Your brand is thriving. It's growing. You can set up shop and stay right there.

Should you be tempted to keep going and chase Mass Influence? I'd be careful about that. In a lot of cases, Mass Influence is actually a step down. Exclusivity and pricing power are highest in the niches. So if you want to keep growing, you might be better off chasing KLT. Too much reach could dilute your brand.

For now, you understand what the Axis looks like. So let's explore how you move through it.

CHAPTER 4

Moving up the Axis

Climbing the Axis of Influence can feel like a grind. That's because it is. Some of the time anyway. And in between the grind, you'll have breakout moments. Or multiple breakout moments. Clear turning points where things change.

Maybe you posted a piece of content that struck a nerve. Maybe you appeared on a podcast or showed up at a specific event. It could be a partnership or even a scandal.

I've researched hundreds of scenarios where things move from Anonymity to Influence. Breakout moments are everywhere. They come through constant repetition and improvement. The moment can last days, weeks, or months. And every breakout moment follows a natural sequence of events.

It starts with reach and then moves to KLT.

Let me repeat that. **First** you must reach someone and **second** they can decide if they want to get to know you, like you, and trust you. It's never the reverse.

Chew on that for a second. It's completely impossible for someone to know, like, or trust you, *before* you've reached them. And once you do reach them, they have two options:

1. They can take in your message and choose to forget all about you. Which is the most common outcome.

2. Or they can take in your message and choose to dig deeper. They Google you, pull you up on Instagram, they text their friends to see if anyone has heard of you. Then they just might go down the rabbit hole and become part of your community.

Again, this can happen in a whirlwind of a few days, or it can take years to percolate.

I'm going to show you what this looks like in real life.

_____

People assume that going from the bottom left to the top right is a straight line. The picture in their head looks like a rocketship, as I've sketched in Diagram 6.

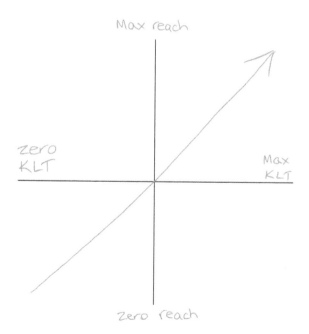

Diagram 6: This is the "straight line" growth people expect.

And that's almost never how it happens in reality.

In real life, you spend a long time in Anonymity. It might feel like a very long time. Then at some point, you break out to the right. And then, if things go well, you go up and to the right. That's when you find some level of influence. It can happen very slowly and then all at once.

I've sketched some more realistic paths in Diagram 7.

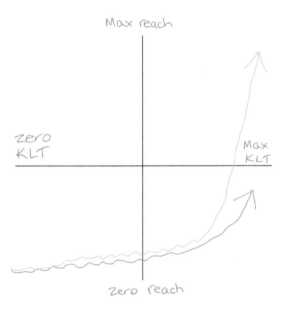

Diagram 7: This is how growth typically looks.

Why is it like this?

Because it takes time to get good at your message. This starts to earn you KLT. It's small at first, but it will grow. And with enough KLT, your message begins to spread. People talk. They share. Word gets around.

Especially when your message forms a part of their identity. It becomes a point of status. A calling card people can use to express their personality.

I'll tell you exactly how to do this in the coming chapters. And how to build your customer community. For now, I just want you to understand why it's so important.

Once you achieve enough KLT, the reach will grow too. But don't rush it. Patience is key.

The time you spend in Anonymity is important. When building a brand, this is the period where you're testing the messaging, seeking validation, tweaking and pivoting, and getting things just right.

We see this all the time in real life.

I want to share a famous example of someone moving through the Axis right in front of our eyes. And this is a powerful example because it was documented for the world to see.

CHAPTER 5

The Speech That Built a Movement

July 27, 2004.

A little-known U.S. Senator takes the stage at the Democratic National Convention. He delivers a rousing 17-minute speech. He discusses his personal background and weaves in classic lessons in American values. He emphasizes unity and hope over division and fear.

In those 17 minutes, he has the attention of America. Even though they've never heard of him, they're listening. And he uses that moment to embed himself in our brains.

His name is Barack Obama. Very few people knew him prior. But his reach suddenly erupted. And in a short period of time, many people decided that he was worth remembering. He became known. And a lot of people decided that they liked him. I'm sure a few even felt they could trust him.

But Obama's story starts long before that moment in 2004. Rewind to 1997, when he served 3 terms in the Illinois Senate. What was he doing between 1997 and 2004? He spent a bunch of that time in Anonymity. At least relatively speaking. Obviously, as a US Senator, some people knew him. But not on a national level.

I didn't know Barack Obama between 1997 and 2004. But I can safely assume he spent that time honing his message, his speaking skills, his public demeanor, and the image he brought to the DNC.

When he hit that stage and delivered the speech, he already had plenty of KLT, even if only from a small group of believers. That's what catapulted him to the stage.

Then he used those 17 minutes of extreme reach to build KLT with a much larger audience. The megaphone was bigger, but the message was the same.

I remember tuning in that night. Here was a charismatic guy with an odd-sounding name. At least for a US politician at the time. And in that moment, a lot of people decided that they knew, liked, and trusted him. The rest is history.

———

Now, I know what you're probably thinking right now.

"Jon, he had a national TV audience back when people actually watched TV. And it was a super high profile event. How could I replicate anything close to this?"

I have two answers:

First, tons of people speak at political conventions all the time. But can you name one other person who has spoken at a political convention in the last 20 years, who wasn't already famous? Seriously. Go ahead. Think of one single name. I'll wait.

Unless you're an even bigger political nerd than me, I'll assume you can't think of anyone. Which makes sense.

Barack Obama was given a high profile opportunity. That's the *reach* component. But he was the one who leveraged that opportunity into true influence. He figured out KLT. He could just as easily have been forgotten 5 minutes later.

Second, I'm using this as my example specifically because it's a famous story. It's an extreme example of the Axis of Influence. Many people can remember this moment. And if you can't, just watch it on YouTube.

Most people won't have a Barack Obama moment. And they definitely don't need one.

This book is about building marketing superpowers for your business. Not becoming President of the United States. Although if you wanted to become President, or build a movement of any kind, this book covers the formula. All I ask is that you use it for good.

———

To recap, your journey through the Axis of Influence starts by honing your craft. You do that in Anonymity. As you get better, your reach will be amplified. And then you develop KLT.

Influence happens when you can offer something that's of value to other people. The right skill at the right moment.

It happens all the time. Breakout songs, iconic speeches, viral videos, popular podcasts, best-selling novels, hit movies, notable gurus, cultural leaders, cult brands, and more. They all follow the Axis of Influence.

Why does this formula matter so much? I'll tell you why. We're going to use it to manufacture an influence machine.

CHAPTER 6

The main character

Now that you understand how the Axis works, we need to choose a main character. Our main character will be the focal point of the brand. They will be the one who actually moves through the Axis.

You might be wondering, why exactly do we need a main character? Isn't my brand the main character of the business?

No.

I might love a coffee shop, but I don't relate to the cup of coffee. I might relate to the owner who runs the place, or the barista behind the counter, or the farmer roasting the beans. But not the coffee.

The main character is central to every story. And in our case, it's central to building influence. The main character is our protagonist. It's the person we're following, learning from, and rooting for. It's impossible to tell a story without it. And it's impossible to build influence without a compelling story.

You might be familiar with terms like "attractive character," "relatable character" and "appealing character". Authors like Seth Godin, Russell Brunson, and Donald Miller use these terms to describe a similar concept.

I call this the *main character*. It's the fuel in the Axis of Influence. The main character is the reason I care. Period.

Just like bands have lead singers. Action movies have heroes. Sports teams have star players. Cereals have mascots. Political campaigns have candidates. Talk shows have hosts.

We need someone to cheer on. We need someone to show up for. We need a leader of our community.

And our sentiment towards the main character will envelope the brand. It's the power of association. That's the essence of brand building.

So the first step in building your brand's influence is answering this question:

Who?

You must figure out who your main character will be.

The good news is there are lots of options. It can be a founder, an executive, a figurehead, a spokesperson, a celebrity, a mascot, or some combination of all those things.

In an owner-operated business, the owner is often the main character who represents the brand. You see this with local car dealerships that run ads featuring "Bargain Bob, the wizard of wheels, whose got dynamite deals this weekend!"

Large companies with outspoken CEO's who appear on news channels and post on social media are the main characters in their corporate brands. These people become celebrities in their own right, keynoting at conferences and penning their own memoirs.

Legendary founders who no longer even work in their businesses day-to-day, will stay onboard purely to be the figurehead of their brand. They have public notoriety and are heavily associated with what they've built.

Cartoon mascots act as the main characters for cereals, insurance companies, and restaurants. Even though they're not real people, they can be very relatable. And they can stick around for generations since they never age or ask for a raise.

Family businesses that are in their third or fourth generation might use a descendant of the founder as the main character. Even though they have no involvement in the business. The goodwill of their name and face alone provide tons of equity to the brand.

Celebrities become the faces of makeup lines, fragrance brands, and credit cards. These celebrity endorsements can become so iconic that sometimes they last for years, with celebrities getting an ownership stake in those businesses.

If you already know who the main character of your brand will be – perfect. You can skip the next chapter.

If not, don't worry at all. You have lots of time to figure it out. In the next chapter, I'll run through the key items I think about when deciding on a main character for a brand.

Hopefully your brain is already jogging through the options.

CHAPTER 7

Choosing the main character

When deciding on your brand's main character, use the MAIN checklist to ensure they are a strong fit.

Mirror

The main character must mirror the target customers. They should be relatable and have relevance to the thing you sell. The target customer should see themselves in the main character. Or see the main character as someone they aspire to be.

Authority

The main character must be able to lead the community. So they need to have some level of authority. In some categories, authority is even more important. If your business operates in pharmaceuticals or advanced technology, authority is essential.

It Factor

The main character needs to attract strangers quickly. Think of this like the "it factor". Hard to describe, but you know it when you see it. It's a certain charisma and magnetism. You just feel better when they're close by. This comes in all varieties. When in doubt, just ask yourself – is this person boring to my target customer? If so, it's a dealbreaker.

Not going anywhere

The main character is a key component of your marketing strategy. And you'll be investing time and resources to build KLT between them and the public. So you need to make sure they're going to stick around and remain interested. And while there are ways to transition from one main character to another, you want to avoid this while in growth mode.

———

That's the MAIN checklist. And it's no wonder that founders and business owners often play the character. They mirror your customers because they know the customer so well. They have authority since they've built a business in the category. They have the it factor since they've been pitching their vision from day one. And they're not going anywhere because a chunk of their net worth is tied up in the fortunes of the company.

If for some reason your company's founder or owner isn't a good fit, go down the list. It could be the CEO or someone from the executive team, a spokesperson, a celebrity, an influencer, an industry thought leader, and even a cartoon mascot.

Whoever you choose as the main character, remember to give it time. Building influence is not a fast process. It can take months or years. There are so many reasons why.

The main character needs to find a public voice and style. Especially if they don't already have a public profile. It's not like you can just start writing or speaking and immediately have perfect delivery. It takes time to truly connect with the public.

It also takes time to become a world-class communicator. Even once you figure out *what* you're going to say, you need to decide *how* you're going to say it. Your words, your phrases, your tone, your language. It all matters. Whether you're writing or speaking, delivery takes time.

And it takes a while for people to find you. You're competing for attention. That's an incredibly valuable and finite asset. So you need to speak lots of times before others catch on.

These are just some of the reasons. There are plenty more. Just understand this. Climbing the Axis takes time. It starts slow. Then people begin to share your message with others. And the KLT compounds. As will the reach. It's worth every moment.

CHAPTER 8

And If You're Still Not Sure…

I know there will be readers who wonder if the main character is necessary. Do I really need a person at the center of my brand? There are so many brands out there who don't. And they do just fine.

It's a fair point. But let me remind you – this book is not called *Average Marketing*. It's called *Marketing Superpowers*. I don't want you competing with others using the same tools and tactics they do. I want your marketing to be so unreasonably effective that competitors can't comprehend how you're doing it.

Think about your favorite movie, or rockstar, or sports team. Whatever it is you're into. Think about how much you like that thing. How much KLT you have for it. A lot, right?

Now compare your KLT for that thing, to the KLT you have towards your favorite brand of toothpaste. Think about it for a moment. I'm guessing there's no comparison. It's kind of a silly question, right?

Exactly.

Those things are all brands. Movies, rockstars, sports teams, and toothpaste. But the first three don't seem like the fourth. It seems like they have an unfair advantage. There are emotions, memories, and feelings tied to those first three things. They have so much more KLT in your mind because they're centered around characters.

The main character.

Because that is what you need to build a marketing superpower.

————

My goal in Section 1 is to break the false belief that influence is random. And since most of the work in marketing is influencing your buyer, you can be sure that success in marketing isn't random either.

It's a series of steps properly planned and executed. And it leads to a natural conclusion: People choose to buy your product.

So now we've covered the path. You know directionally where you are today and where you want to go. Next we'll cover the *how*.

I'm going to lay out a specific formula you'll use to move through the Axis of Influence. To bring people along with you. And to turn many of those people into paying customers.

————

Section 1: Recap

- Becoming popular is not complicated. It follows a simple path, but not a straight path.
- The Axis of Influence has 2 factors: reach on the Y axis and KLT (known, liked, trusted) on the X axis.
- There are four quadrants: Anonymity, Mass Influence, 15 Minutes of Fame, and Niche Influence.
  - *Anonymity* is the starting point. This is where almost everyone begins and it's crucial for testing, tweaking, and building skills
  - *Mass Influence* is the top-right quadrant where the most well-known and trusted figures reside.
  - *15 Minutes of Fame* is what happens when you gain reach rapidly without much KLT. It usually results in a quick crash.
  - Niche Influence is where 95% of the action is. This is where the most valuable brands often live.
- Patience is key – breakout moments follow a natural sequence of reach first, then KLT.
- You must find a main character who can connect with your target customer.
- Use the MAIN checklist: Mirror, Authority, It Factor, and Not Going Anywhere.
- Give your main character time to blossom. The reach and KLT will compound. That's how you climb the Axis of Influence.

Bonus material

I sketched all the diagrams in Section 1 myself. I hope these visuals help you grasp how things get popular on the Axis of Influence. I actually have these sketches printed out on my desk so I can reference them anytime I want. It reminds me that brand building takes time. And I can plot out where my brand is on the Axis as I build.

If you want to do the same thing, you can grab PDF versions for free at JonDavids.com/MarketingSuperpowers.

Or snap the QR code below:

SECTION 2

Creating Your Movement

CHAPTER 9

Why most influencers aren't influencing anyone

As CEO of Influicity, I'm exposed to lots of people who call themselves "influencers". Thousands. We work with them on marketing programs for our clients.

- 20 YouTubers promoting a new car

- 45 TikTokers doing restaurant reviews

- 200 Instagrammers showcasing a new video game console

We do this every day.

Now ask me if I've ever heard of any of these influencers. The answer is usually no. Most of the time, I have no idea who they are. No offense to them. I'm sure they're all talented. There are just so many of them. And I'm only talking about the ones we actually work with.

What about the ones we don't work with? There are millions. Literally millions. They're visiting our website, emailing us, cold calling, and direct messaging. The @influicity account on Instagram gets messages every day from people who would love to work with our clients.

And I respect the hustle. These people are working hard to gain attention on the internet. But let's be real. Most of them are not really influencers. In fact, they're not influencing anyone about anything.

The world of influencers is crowded. I've had a front row seat for a decade. And there are more people calling themselves "influencers" every day.

So what does this have to do with your marketing? A lot. Stick with me, I'll explain.

The Problem with Influencers

Influencers. Content creators. Social media stars. There are many names for it. But ultimately, it's the same thing. These people are putting stuff out on social media and reaching lots of followers. But what does that even mean?

Are they making content? Yes. Are they getting likes? Sure. Are they influencing people? No. Not even a little bit. At least most of them aren't.

Influence is a complicated thing. Even people who are considered influential are quite limited in their influence. They may only influence a select group of people. Within that group, they may only influence those people some of the time. And that influence with those people at those times will work at different levels, depending on the topic, the rationale, and how receptive they are in the moment.

But it goes even deeper than that.

So many people building audiences on social media are literally just filling the feeds. Spraying their socials. Throwing up content that the algorithm likes and hoping to hack engagement. Their stuff is not creative. Or profound. Or original. Or entertaining. Or inspiring. Or educational.

It's nothing.

Let's be clear. I'm not saying any of this to be mean. I don't want to discourage people in their creative pursuits. I'm just being real. It's not groundbreaking content. And I want to make sure you don't fall into that trap. If you want your main character and your brand to stand out in a sea of "influence", it needs to be downright spectacular. Thumb-stopping. It needs to leave a mark.

And it needs to have a higher meaning.

I'm going to teach you how to do that. And we're going to take lessons from the top 1% of influencers.

CHAPTER 10

Lessons from the Influencer Class

Instead of trying to make content, you need to *create a movement*. And fuel that movement with your content. When I say movement, I'm actually trying to move people from one place to another. Ideally, towards my belief. It's the one thing I'm trying to push. It's the core of my brand promise. And it's represented by my main character.

That movement doesn't need to be lofty or even serious. It just needs to relate to your area of expertise and your brand.

- If you make fruity bubble gum, your movement could be about how amazing fruity bubble gum is. Much better than mint.

- If you sell smart irrigation systems, your movement is about how people need to stop wasting water and upgrade their lawn care technology.

- If you're a real estate agent in Boston, your movement is about how fantastic it is to live in Boston. After all, you want people to move there. (Literally.)

As you can see, these don't need to be serious or heavy topics. Not curing diseases, stopping wars, or eliminating crime. We're doing simple things. You are creating a core belief in something and getting others to believe it with you.

Do you see how thinking about it as a movement can help you focus your message? And become more influential in the process? That's what this is all about.

But I know that creating a movement can still seem lofty. It's difficult to know where to start. That's why I created a formula to make it simple. I call it the Movement Formula.

CHAPTER 11

The Movement Formula

There are 3 factors behind every movement.

1. A <u>unifying belief</u> that enhances [good thing] or reduces [bad thing]

2. <u>Faith</u> that this is the best way to do it

3. <u>Actions</u> towards achieving that thing

When you have those 3 ingredients, you have a movement.

Let's look at this formula another way:

Unifying Belief that enhances (good thing) or reduces (bad thing)

X

Faith that this is the best way to do it

=

Action towards acheiving that thing

You start with a unifying belief that people can get behind and multiply it by giving people faith in that unifying belief. The strength of that belief and the faith behind it equals the action those people take. And by "action" I mean sales. After all, they'll take action in your movement by buying the thing you're selling.

The reason that the unifying belief is *multiplied* by faith is simple: If there's zero faith, the belief is worthless. If there's a little bit of faith, the belief will be minimal. If you can multiply faith by 10, or 100, or 1,000, the belief will be off the charts. More importantly, the action will follow in exact proportion. That's what happens with world-class movements. They can literally alter culture and society. This is very simple math. And I'm really not good at math. So if I get this, you certainly can too.

Let's look at each ingredient more closely.

1. A unifying belief that enhances [good thing] or reduces [bad thing]

Being an influencer is about getting others to believe the thing you tell them. Within that they need to know you, like you, and trust you. And to win them over you'll need to offer something that gives them more of what they want (i.e. a good thing) or eliminates something they hate (i.e. a bad thing).

If I'm a travel agent who helps people plan exotic vacations, and you're someone who loves exotic vacations, then my unifying belief helps you enhance your "good thing" – taking exotic vacations. If I'm a cyber security expert who helps people avoid data breaches, and you're someone who wants to avoid data breaches, then my unifying belief helps you reduce your "bad thing" – a data breach.

If I'm a math tutor who teaches you how to solve difficult math equations, then my unifying belief helps you increase your "good thing" – being good at math.

These are all clear examples of enhancing a good thing or reducing a bad thing. That is effectively what a movement is all about.

And notice that the unifying belief is something that your target audience wants. That doesn't mean *everyone* wants it. Some people may not be interested in exotic vacations, or data breaches, or being good at math. In fact, some people might be against those things. For all sorts of reasons.

Movements rarely have universally held beliefs. Rather, they unite under a set of beliefs that one group of passionate people can get behind. But not everyone.

Think about cultural touch points like sports, music and politics. One thing that drives fans to be passionate about their "team" is that there are so many detractors. People who are against the movement. They might also have an opposing movement.

The key is to appeal to the people that you want to target. Who is your target customer? Don't worry about all the people who don't share your belief. With any luck, they'll become vocal haters and drive more growth for you, by rallying the believers.

I'll talk about the importance of haters in Section 8. But for now, just understand, haters are a good thing for your movement.

This is absolutely not supposed to be a "universal" belief. It is a "unifying belief". There's a big difference.

2. Faith that this is the best way to do it

Once you've established the unifying belief, you must instill faith that this is the way. Faith can be challenging because it's illogical.

Faith is belief without hard evidence. In the case of a travel agent who plans exotic vacations, there's no proof that this particular travel agent is the best in the world. After all, what does "best" even mean? And if there were an agreed upon definition, how would we evaluate that? I obviously can't speak to every travel agent in the world.

This goes back to the main character at the core. If they've done an effective job building KLT, then the brand has a good shot at instilling faith.

There are also varying degrees of faith. Some people are devout without question. Some are constantly questioning. And their faith deepens or weakens over time. You need to always be pushing faith forward. It's the glue that holds your movement together.

3. Actions towards achieving that unifying belief

Once you have a unifying belief that multiplies with faith, the last step is action. What action can your believers take to achieve that outcome?

Let's go back to my examples from before.

If I'm the travel agent pushing exotic vacations, believers can take action by going to those locations. Tasting the food. Drinking the wine. Breathing the air.

If I'm the cybersecurity expert pushing data protection, people can take action by using strong passwords, software updates, running backups, and using multi-factor authentication.

If I'm the tutor pushing math education, people can take action by taking courses, practicing the equations, collaborative learning, writing tests, and applying math to their work.

But remember, each of these people is selling their solution. Travel, cyber security, math education. That's the product. That's the revenue. That's why the movement exists. Once you create the unifying belief and multiply it with faith, the only logical step is to sell the solution.

We need to give people something to do. And make it accessible for them to take action. After all, if I'm the main character with a movement behind me, I want people to move. To go from point A to point B. And of course, as a marketer, I want this movement to drive sales.

Those 3 ingredients make up the Movement Formula.

Unifying Belief x Faith = Action

Now let's look at some powerful movements and see how they use the Movement Formula.

CHAPTER 12

Movements All Around Us

Lasting movements are all around us. Some of these have been around for years, decades, or centuries. To be clear, these are not single company movements. I'm using these as examples to show you how effective and timeless they are.

Example #1: The Ketogenic Diet

1. Unifying belief that enhances [good thing] or reduces [bad thing]

Consume less carbs, eat more fat and protein, and you'll lose weight.

2. Faith that this is the best way to do it

- Celebrities and athletes who follow the Keto diet like Halle Berry, Kim Kardashian, Lebron James, Tim Tebow, and others.

- Health and medical influencers who talk about Keto like Dr. Josh Axe and Dr. Eric Berg.

- Food companies who develop Keto friendly foods making it easier for people to adopt this style of eating.

3. Actions towards achieving that unifying belief

- Eat lots of meat, eggs, and vegetables

- Avoid grains, sugars, and processed foods

- Limit your carbohydrate intake

- Follow a meal plan

According to UC Davis, the global addressable market for the Keto Diet is $11-12 billion in 2022. That's a whole lot of avocado-oil mayonnaise, high-fiber tortillas, and protein cookies. If you're a believer in the Keto Diet, you'll take action by purchasing these products.

Notice how the Keto Diet combines a powerful unifying belief with faith-building validation. There's plenty of action people can take to follow the movement, including buying lots of stuff tailor-made for them. Nothing helps you express belief quite like a dollar.

This is a clear example of a movement in action.

Let's look at another one.

Example #2: Value Investing

1. Unifying belief that enhances [good thing] or reduces [bad thing]

Buy stocks that are trading for less than their intrinsic value and make more money.

2. Faith that this is the best way to do it

- Famous value investors like Benjamin Graham and Warren Buffett

- Dedicated investment funds and vehicles

- Decades of evidence for its success

- Books and courses on this topic

- Social media discussion and debate around the topic

3. Actions towards achieving that unifying belief

- Evaluating stocks based on value investing principles

- Reading financial reports

- Investing with a margin of safety

- Putting your money in value investing funds

Value investing touches on something that most people want. To make more money and lose less money. It uses that motivation to create a simple unifying belief.

Anyone who is moved by this unifying belief can read countless books and articles on the topic. This will strengthen their belief and faith in the value investing approach.

As for action, there's a lot of it. You can certainly invest your own money and follow the guidelines of value investing. Or you can entrust your cash with an investment fund whose focus is on value investing. These come in all flavors, with names like small-cap value funds, dividend value funds, quantitative value funds, and so on.

You can be sure there are plenty of money managers who are getting paid to handle your money. All thanks to the movement of value investing.

And now let's look at the mother of all movements. Get ready — this is a big one.

Example #3: Organized Religion

1. Unifying belief that enhances [good thing] or reduces [bad thing]

Follow the teachings of God and you'll go to heaven.

2. *Faith that this is the best way to do it*

- Prominent religious leaders throughout society

- Compelling stories, characters, and lessons

- Visibility in media and entertainment

- Schools and educational programs

- Family traditions and rituals

3. *Actions towards achieving that unifying belief*

- Go to church, temple, etc.

- Give to charity

- Don't steal

- Be kind to your neighbors

Religion is my favorite example of a movement. Because it was likely the earliest and most enduring movement in human existence. I'm not referring to any one religion specifically, but religion more broadly. And because it is taught in society from such an early age, it resonates with people more strongly than almost any other movement.

The unifying belief is simple and clear. Humans have a great desire to find purpose in their life. Wondering about the meaning of it all. What happens before we're born or after we die? What is the difference between good and evil? How can we serve a higher purpose?

Religion has it all.

Faith is instilled in people early and often. And there is plenty of action to take if you are a religious person.

As an example, let's look at the Catholic Church. I'm using this only because there's a good amount of public information on the money involved in the Catholic Church. And we're talking about lots of money.

It's hard to quantify exactly how much money the Catholic Church generates. The tithe alone is worth a ton. That's where every member of a church donates 10% of their income to the church. But it gets much bigger than that.

A report by Yale Climate Connections in 2021 reveals that the Catholic Church owns 177 million acres of land across the globe for its churches and schools, along with farmland and forest land.

There's big money in this movement. And it's been around for a couple thousand years. That's serious staying power.

And it goes even further. The most iconic movements encourage people to take action together. Sports teams have stadiums. Politicians have rallies. And religions have temples. Bringing people together amplifies the unifying belief and the faith. That all leads to more action.

Let's look at some of the deeper elements of religion and what makes it such a powerful example of the Movement Formula.

CHAPTER 13

Movement Power Moves

Sticking with the example of religion, there are some specific things that they do to drive the movement forward. I call these the "Movement Power Moves." And here are some of my favorites.

1. Rituals - birth ceremonies, coming of age passages, etc.

2. Gathering places - temples, churches, mosques, shrines, etc.

3. Heroes - gods, deities, prophets, angels, etc.

4. Villains - the devil, the serpent, etc.

5. Rewards - going to heaven, being a moral person, etc.

6. Punishment - purgatory, being shunned by your community, etc.

The most powerful movements copy some or many of these Movement Power Moves. Straight from the religion playbook.

- They have rituals like how you open the box or the sound of the product.

- They have gathering places like conferences and industry parties.

- They deify their leaders, creating epic stories, more fitting of gods than humans.

- They create bad guys, usually from their competition.

- They reward you with their product, new features, upgrades, and bonuses.

- They punish you with reminders of what you're missing.

———

Take a close look at that list. Does any particular brand pop into mind that uses these Movement Power Moves?

Probably a few.

But I'll give you one: Apple.

It dominates the Movement Formula along with all the Movement Power Moves.

They've been doing it for years. It looks like this:

1. Unifying belief that enhances [good thing] or reduces [bad thing]

Technology is beautiful and powerful. And we do it better than anyone.

2. Faith that this is the best way to do it

- Tech leaders who swear by the brand

- Iconic Apple events

- Busy Apple stores

- Legendary Apple commercials

- Steve Jobs

3. Actions towards achieving that unifying belief

- Hold the world in your hand with iPhone

- Put every song in your pocket with iTunes

- Run all your devices with iOS

- Stay in touch with iMessage

- Place the world on your wrist with Apple Watch

- Keep your data safe on iCloud

- Find what you love with AirTag

- Listen to everything with AirPods

As you can see, Apple is more than a business. It's more than a brand. It's a movement. Complete with the Movement Formula and all the Power Moves.

They start with a unifying belief that we can all rally behind. They ramp up our faith with a continuous stream of icons, influencers, heroes, villains, rituals, and more. Then they let us take action by delivering industry-defining products.

Unifying belief to faith to action. And the first company to a $1 trillion dollar valuation.

CHAPTER 14

Using Your Movement to Sell Stuff

In Part 2 of this book, I'll go much deeper into each piece of the Movement Formula. So if it's still percolating in your head, that's cool. These concepts took me years to formulate. And I'm still learning new things everyday as we put them into practice for clients.

So far we've discussed the key elements of your movement in the Movement Formula. Along with some extra ways to drive your movement forward, using the Power Moves.

But how does all this fit into your company? How do you apply it to your strategy in a way that's simple and logical?

I designed the Movement Formula specifically to grow businesses. If you want to start a political movement or a social movement, the process would probably be similar. But that's not my game. I'm a business builder and marketing practitioner at heart. I take businesses from small sales to big sales. That's where my focus is.

So let's look at the Movement Formula through a purely commercial lens. It looks like this:

1. *Unifying belief is your <u>marketing</u>*

2. *Faith is <u>proving</u> your results*

3. *Action is <u>selling</u> your stuff*

Your marketing is an expression of your unifying belief. Faith is the proof that backs up the unifying belief. And action is selling your product or service.

Are you seeing how this all ties back to growth?

The action is commerce. It's money. It's everything.

But before we can make any of this happen, we need to lay the foundation for your brand. We'll do that with a captivating story. That's coming up next.

Quick side note – I hope you're learning a ton and having fun so far. If so, I have one quick request. If you feel you're getting some value, head over to Amazon and leave a review for this book. It doesn't need to be a long review or a perfect review. Just a sentence or two about what you've learned so far.

Head over to JonDavids.com/bookreview to leave a review right now.

Okay, let's get back to the book.

———

Section 2: Recap

- The Movement Formula has 3 components:
    - A unifying belief that enhances [good thing] or reduces [bad thing]
    - Faith that this is the best way to do it
    - Actions towards achieving that thing
- The Movement Formula is unifying belief x faith = action
- You can enhance your movement with Power Moves. For example, rituals, gathering places, heroes, villains, rewards, and punishment.
- Another way to think about it is
    - Unifying belief is your marketing
    - Faith is demonstrated by your results
    - Action is selling your product

Bonus material:

I made a special worksheet that breaks down the Movement Formula and the Power Moves. It's really simple and you can use it as a quick reference whenever you need it.

Grab it now at JonDavids.com/MarketingSuperpowers.

Or snap the QR code below:

SECTION 3

The Foundation

CHAPTER 15

How I became an entrepreneur

I built a business making $300,000 a year in college. And I started with zero knowledge and zero money.

Let me tell you exactly how I did it.

Rewind to 2003. I'm a kid who loves entrepreneurship and has a knack for marketing. So naturally, I start an internet company. It's an online magazine. Basically a fancy blog. To get it off the ground, I need to figure out 3 things:

1. How to create content

2. How to build an audience

3. How to make money

Let's go deeper into each one.

For content, I settle on lifestyle articles - travel, pets, fashion, and so on. But I need to find writers who can make this content. I reach out to my school's journalism department and ask if they'll send an email to all the students. Tell them there's a publication looking for writers.

They agree. Within 24 hours, I get 100 applications and hire 10. Then I hire one more to be the editor, in charge of all the others.

I tell them I'll pay if I ever make money at this. They don't care. It's solid experience. Now I have content but I need to find an audience. This is gonna be a mission.

There's no Instagram. No TikTok. No YouTube. The biggest sites in the world are called MSN, AOL, and Yahoo. I need to get my content seen on those sites. But how?

I spend the next 2 months hunting down the editors of these portals and finally connect with the guy who runs MSN. Let's call him Stan. I tell Stan about my awesome blog and ask if I can post my content to MSN. He politely explains that his content comes from The New York Times and ESPN. Stan's not interested.

"Ok, thanks" I say, and hang up.

For the next 6 months, I email Stan every single week. Let me repeat: Every. Single. Week.

I send him ideas, suggestions, stats, and samples. I'm relentless. He totally ignores me. Until one morning.

I check my inbox to find a message from Stan. MSN is launching a pets section and they need content now. Can I send 20 articles this week?

Hell yeah!

"How much will it cost?" he asks.

"Nothing," I reply. "Just put my brand name on every article with links back to my site." Basically, I want free ads and a lot of them. This is gonna be my traffic fire hose.

"Done," he says.

One week later, we're up on MSN. In a flash, my little blog hits a million readers. I can't believe I'm gonna pull this off. Just one more thing to do.

The next day, I sign up for Google AdSense and paste the javascript up on my site. The most profitable 4 lines of code ever written. And just like that, I'm making $822 a day.

And that was the start of my entrepreneurial journey.

––––––––

Pretty good story, right? In case you're wondering, that's my origin story. And it's 100% true. I've told it thousands of times. And I've gotten better at telling it along the way.

And I've got different versions of the story too. Long versions, short versions, written versions, video versions. I have a version I tell on stage and a version I tell when I'm being interviewed. In the context of entrepreneurship, it's the very foundation of who I am. It's the myth. It's the magic. It's the story I tell over and over again to cement my credibility.

Once you hear it, you immediately feel more connected to me. If you're an entrepreneur, you probably appreciate my hustle. You have more trust in what I say.

Even if you're not an entrepreneur, hopefully you're rooting for me from the sidelines.

I'm pretty sure you are. Because I've told this origin story to millions of people. On my podcast, on social media, in my emails, and at events. I've tweaked it, polished it, and memorized it. I've crafted every single word to maximize the impact on the listener.

I have a short version, a long version, a written version, and a spoken version. I've got a 30 minute video on YouTube that people love. You can go watch it yourself at _JonDavids.com/originstory_

I've seen the reactions up close. This story tells you that I'm the real deal. That's what an origin story is all about.

And that's why your brand needs one too.

CHAPTER 16

Origin Stories

Your brand needs an origin story. And the origin story should center around your main character.

Think about every superhero you know. Batman, Superman, Spiderman, Ironman. They all have origin stories. These narratives are essential to the events that follow. They give us context, expectations, and belief for what comes next.

Bruce Wayne witnesses his parents murdered as a child, driving him to dedicate his life to fighting crime. He becomes the vigilante caped crusader known as Batman.

Kal-El is born on planet Krypton, but sent to Earth and raised as Clark Kent. There he discovers his worldly powers, using them to fight for good over evil as Superman.

Peter Parker is bitten by a radioactive spider, giving him superhuman abilities. He uses them to battle the bad guys as Spider-Man.

Tony Stark is a billionaire inventor who is captured by terrorists. He narrowly escapes by building a suit of powered armor and transforms into the crime fighter, Iron Man.

Each of these origin stories is modeled on the hero's journey. It's a tried and true formula that's been recycled for centuries. The modern version was popularized by Joseph Campbell, an American mythologist and writer.

I've seen versions of the hero's journey with 17 steps ranging up to 25 steps.

And I created my own version, which I've used to help 100's of brands and people develop their own origin stories. It's called the *Origin-8* Framework. (Pronounced "originate" but spelled with the number eight. Do you get it?)

And don't worry – you don't need to be a crime fighting vigilante superhero to have a great origin story. Not even close.

In the next chapter, I'll break down all the pieces of a mighty origin story and teach you exactly how to create one for your main character and your brand.

CHAPTER 17

The Origin-8 Framework

The *Origin-8* Framework has 8 ingredients. Each one builds on the last. Together they tell a complete story of where the main character comes from, how they earned their battle scars, and the superpower they obtained as a result.

The 8 ingredients are:

1. Ordinary World

2. Struggle

3. Rock bottom

4. Enlightenment

5. Exit comfort zone

6. Ordeal

7. Reward

8. Superpower

Let's look at each one more closely. As we do, I want you to think through your own version. If you are your own main character, this should be easy. If you're building this story for a larger brand, put yourself in the mind of the main character and imagine how they would experience each step. If it's easier, grab a pen and paper and jot down your thoughts as we move along.

Don't worry if you can't clearly identify one exact item for each of the 8 steps. For now, just think through the possibilities. Afterwards, we'll craft the full story. And we'll transform your main character into a legendary superhero.

For easy reading, I'm going to write the 8 steps as though you are the main character. But it's all the same if it's someone else.

1. Ordinary World

This is where our main character started. It's the beginning of your movie. That doesn't mean we need to go back to the womb. Our goal is to tell a story that starts at the beginning of this journey.

So in the context of your business or brand, the Ordinary World is what you were like just before starting that business. Or it could be what you were like before you attained the skill that eventually led to your business.

2. Struggle

When did you realize things weren't quite right? Maybe this was something internal like being unhappy with a job. Or an external event, like an unhealthy relationship or a crummy experience. Maybe it was a big move or a medical issue or a bad habit you just couldn't break.

It might also be a series of related struggles that add up to a big one. Like if you continued to fail at a certain task over and over again. It might have even been over the course of a few months or years.

3. Rock bottom

What was the decisive last moment of that struggle? The event that made you realize that you needed to take massive action? That the status quo simply wasn't going to work anymore.

Again, in real life this event isn't always a single moment. So it's okay to chain a few events together. After all, the alcoholic who enters rehab might need to check into that same rehab facility 28 times before they make a life change. Don't get caught up in exact dates or times. Just think of events more broadly.

4. Enlightenment

This is your moment of enlightenment. When the dust cleared after your rock bottom, what was that glimpse of clarity? It could have been an external force, like a friend or mentor. Or maybe it came from a voice inside you, through a moment of self-discovery.

Similar to rock bottom, the Enlightenment event appears really clearly in movies. The protagonist usually looks around like they can't believe they've just uncovered the truth. Music swells telling the audience that our hero has been awakened. Your enlightenment might not look this euphoric in reality. But don't worry. We'll polish it up before long.

5. Exit Comfort Zone

Now comes the real work. You've struggled, hit rock bottom, and emerged through a moment of enlightenment. It's time for you to engage your demons. Unlock your truth. Unleash the beast inside you. Exiting your comfort zone is essential for growth. It means doing the thing you've never done before. So if you've managed to achieve anything, certainly you have moved out of your comfort zone.

Let's capture that moment and describe what it felt like.

6. Ordeal

It's not supposed to be easy. It's supposed to be worth it. And that's why there must be an ordeal.

You exited your comfort zone and then something happened. Was there a battle? A learning curve? Something you had to do to earn your stripes?

I'm sure there was. What was that ordeal and how did you conquer it?

7. Reward

Now you've gone through the ordeal and made peace with the demons. What was the reward awaiting you on the other side? This could have been a lesson or an insight. Or it might have been more concrete like a giant bag of money.

If you were battling weight loss, the reward might have been achieving your ideal weight. If you were training to be a mountain climber, the reward could be you scaling to the summit.

The reward is simply the pot of gold awaiting you at the end of the rainbow.

8. Superpower

With reward in hand, you now have the superpower. The experience has given you a life lesson that is yours forever. You've earned it.

You can use it to spread the word. You have the authority and credibility to do so. Because you lived it. No one can take that away from you.

Now we have all the pieces. Let's look at a famous Origin Story using the *Origin-8* Framework. We'll take my favorite Origin Story of all time.

CHAPTER 18

I'm Batman

I love the story of Batman. He is my favorite superhero of all time. And one of my favorite movies of all time is Christopher Nolan's *Batman Begins*, the telling of Batman's origin story.

Let's look at Batman's origin story through the Origin-8 Framework. To be clear, I'm not going to tell you the exact version from *Batman Begins*, but rather a compilation based on the multiple versions of this story that have been told over the decades.

1. Ordinary World - Bruce Wayne is a rich kid living a privileged life in Gotham City. His parents, Thomas and Martha Wayne are high society fixtures. Respected and admired. But Gotham can be a dangerous place.

2. Struggle - One night after leaving the theater through a back alleyway, Thomas and Martha are murdered during a mugging gone wrong. Bruce witnesses this traumatic event. It has a profound impact on him.

3. Rock bottom - Bruce is alone, isolated, and scared. He considers killing the man who murdered his parents. But he won't let his anger consume him. Instead he chooses to forget the life he knows.

4. Enlightenment - Our hero flees Gotham City, abandons his identity, and sets out to find purpose. On his travels, he meets Ra's Al Ghul, a man who provides young Bruce with structure and purpose, to channel his rage.

5. Exit comfort zone - Bruce enters Ra's Al Ghul's training and learns how to fight. He studies the ways of the warrior. And he reflects on how to become more than a mere man. How to become a symbol of light, within a sea of darkness.

6. Ordeal - Through this intense training, Bruce acquires the skills to become a vigilante fighter. But Ra's Al Ghul wants more. He wants Bruce to be an assassin. Our hero refuses and narrowly escapes before Ra's Al Ghul can kill him.

7. Reward - Bruce returns home, a changed man. With new skills and a renewed purpose in life, our hero has found his calling and a true purpose. He is no longer the spoiled rich kid but a battle-hardened crime fighter.

8. Superpower - I'm Batman. (Say it like you mean it.)

———

You see how that works? It all comes together in my simple *Origin-8* Framework.

But I know what you're thinking. These are all highly dramatic events. There's money, murder, mischief, martial arts. So of course you can make an origin story sound interesting.

What about an ordinary life? How can I make that sound interesting?

I'm going to show you right now.

CHAPTER 19

Creating Your Main Character's Origin Story

Let's go in the opposite direction. We'll take a perfectly ordinary person and give them an extraordinary origin story. I want you to see how easy it can be, regardless of the circumstances.

Afterwards, I'll give you a full breakdown so you can create an origin story for yourself.

Stacey, the Travel Agent

Let's say you have a travel consulting business. And you want to develop an origin story that tells people where your passion comes from. It might look like this:

1. Ordinary World - I was born in a small town. I never even flew on an airplane until I was 20 years old.

2. Struggle - My friends all traveled to Europe the summer after high school. But I had no money and no job. So I couldn't afford to go with them.

3. Rock bottom - I missed out. And I felt like a loser. These years were supposed to be special. Making memories to last a lifetime. Instead, I was wasting away.

4. Enlightenment - And then I saw it. A limited time travel offer, to visit Croatia for only $1,500. If I got a job right now, I could save that much over the summer.

5. Exit Comfort Zone - I worked my butt off, stashed away the money, and booked a 1-way ticket to Croatia. All by myself. No turning back now.

6. Ordeal - I landed with $200 in my pocket. I was terrified. But I found a hostel to stay in, made fast friends, and remained there for 3 months.

7. Reward - It was so much fun. I ended up traveling for the rest of that year. City to city. I had the time of my life. I took buses, trains, and boats. I even hitchhiked. I became a travel aficionado.

8. Superpower - I can plan any dream travel experience.

———

Notice that this is a very simple story and job. Stacey isn't a crime fighting superhero. Stacey is a travel agent. Someone who can book airfare and hotels on your behalf.

But that story really hits home, doesn't it?

It makes you feel connected to Stacey. Like you're on the journey with her. You're rooting for her to win. Why is that?

Let's break it down further to see how I constructed this story for maximum impact.

CHAPTER 20

5 Rules for Maximum Impact Origin Stories

Have you ever read a book and then watched the movie version? And as you're watching it on screen, all you can think about is how this character is different, that scene was added, this event was missing, this part happened before that part, and so on.

It's weird.

As if they took a book you loved, threw it in a blender and served up some twisted literary cocktail. Not better or worse. Just different.

You know why they do that? Because they need to keep it interesting! So they switch timelines, cut characters, squish multiple events, chop scenes, and more.

All tricks of the trade.

And these are tricks you need to know if you're going to write a strong origin story.

I've narrowed it down to 5 rules you must follow.

1. You can tie events together creatively

When writing about stories that we know very well, we tend to get bogged down in cause and effect. We remind ourselves that thing "A" happened because of thing "B", not because of thing "C". But when you're telling an origin story, you need to loosen up on cause and effect.

I'm not suggesting you should lie, but you can certainly create a narrative around things that happened, even if these things were not directly connected.

For example, did Stacey really miss the trip with her friends after high school because she couldn't afford it? Maybe she had something else going on at that time. Or maybe she just didn't want to travel to the place her friends were going. Or maybe she got into a fight with her friend the day before and didn't feel like traveling. Or maybe she just slept in and missed the flight.

My thought is, who cares? We're not writing a play-by-play. We're not under oath. We're composing a great origin story. And each part of the narrative conveys a specific message.

When crafting Stacey's story, I decided to build the reason around money. Because it's simple and relatable. Struggling with money is something most people encounter in their life. It ties in nicely with the "Rock Bottom" and the "Enlightenment" pieces of the story.

Also, I may be trying to position Stacey as someone who can help you travel on a budget. So making it about money helps me drive that point forward.

Little things like words, phrases, and ideas within the origin story can point towards a larger theme. Bringing you closer to the subject. So we need to orchestrate it in just the right way.

Let's say, for example, that Stacey is not a travel agent, but instead she's a financial advisor. And we want to position this as an origin story for how she became a financial advisor. Steps 1-5 might be the same (Ordinary World, Struggle, Rock Bottom, Enlightenment, and Exit Comfort Zone).

But for Step 6 (Ordeal), we could go into detail about how Stacey learned how to manage her finances, as opposed to planning her travel.

Then for Step 7 (Reward), we could talk about how she learned to become financially secure. And finally for Step 8 (Superpower), we would say that she now knows all about financial planning.

You see how we can essentially use the same story to make two different points? It's because we are tying unrelated events together creatively.

Don't get caught up in "the truth, the whole truth, and nothing but the truth". Focus on the narrative. Tell a logical version of the story. It is your story after all.

2. Don't get hung up on timelines

Did Stacey already have a job when she reached the Enlightenment stage? Or did she get the job afterwards?

Did her friends travel to Europe the summer after high school? Or did they actually go a few years earlier?

The answer is, it doesn't matter. We're telling a story about things that actually happened. If you need to adjust sequences to make the story flow, or to ensure events make sense, then just swap the timelines.

When you watch a movie based on a true story, do you ever notice how it says "based on true events" and not "this movie is an exact reenactment of true events?"

This is why.

Because timelines get shifted. It's an important device in storytelling. Similar to tying unrelated events together, swapping the sequence of events lets you tell a better story.

And that's what this is all about.

3. It's okay to play up and/or omit items

When we go back through our memory, we may recall all sorts of details. Probably far more than is necessary to use in our story. We also may feel like certain events are less important. Like they didn't have a big impact on what happened.

When you're developing an origin story, you need to craft the series of events in a way that best communicates the story. That's the goal.

In the case of Stacey, I said that she landed with $200 in her pocket, found a hostel to stay in, made fast friends, and remained in Croatia for 3 months.

In reality, maybe she had $10,000 in her bank account, but she only had $200 of cash physically in her pocket. Maybe she had reserved a room at the hostel before she left. So she knew that she was heading there once she landed. Maybe she had a friend of a friend who was also staying at that hostel. So she was able to make new friends instantly.

All these things are possible. And I didn't say anything to contradict these possibilities. But we don't need to mention any of it. Because it doesn't matter. It's irrelevant. These extra details reduce the drama and dull the story.

I'm trying to tell the story in the most compelling way.

When crafting your brand's origin story, you can slice and dice to keep the narrative tight and powerful.

4. Simple is better

As with all copywriting, the goal is to keep it simple. Tell people what series of events led the main character to where they are now. Don't complicate it with other characters, multiple plotlines, confusing events, or anything that could throw your reader off course.

For example, I'm sure Stacey's friends have names but I'm not mentioning them. Because they are irrelevant to the story. They're non-player characters.

I also said she had a job, but I didn't mention where she worked. Again, it doesn't drive the story forward. So including it would just take up space.

The goal is to draw in your audience and build KLT. Anything that detracts from that hinders your story. It gets in the way.

When in doubt, always keep it simple.

5. Be human, not superhuman

In order to be relatable, the main character needs to be vulnerable. This is where so many people miss the mark. When telling their story, they want to come off as perfect and flawless. Never showing the kinks in their armor.

This is the wrong way to go because it makes the main character look flat and boring. Think about the superhero stories. There's always vulnerability.

Batman has loved ones, like Alfred and Robin. He is human and therefore has human limitations. He depends on technology, which can betray him. Imagine how boring the adventures of Batman would be if he lacked vulnerabilities.

Superman has Kryptonite. Spiderman's Spider-Sense's can mislead him. Iron Man relies on a manmade suit.

These are all vulnerabilities.

Give your character texture. Vulnerabilities provide a sense of tension and challenge within the adventure.

Be human. Not superhuman.

––––––––

That's the *Origin-8* Framework. Use it to create a foundation for your main character that fans can latch onto. It will bring your brand to life on a whole new level.

As I say to founders and executives who are the heroes of their own story: Forget who you were. Become the person you were meant to be. And share it with the world.

But don't do it yet. Because we're just getting started.

The Origin Story is the beginning of your narrative. Next we're going to sharpen your story-telling abilities so you can deliver a message that leaves a dent.

––––––––

Section 3: Recap

- A powerful origin story is a critical part of your brand narrative.
- Strong origin stories follow the hero's journey
- You can use my Origin-8 Framework to build your own
  a. Ordinary World
  b. Struggle
  c. Rock Bottom
  d. Enlightenment
  e. Exit Comfort Zone
  f. Ordeal
  g. Reward
  h. Superpower
- Any character can have a powerful origin story
- For effective story-telling, remember these tips:
  o Tie events together creatively
  o Don't get hung up on timelines
  o Play up and omit Items as necessary
  o Simple is better
  o Be human, not superhuman

Bonus material:

I put this all into a worksheet with the Origin-8 Formula and a few examples. You can use it as a quick reference as you craft your own origin story.

Grab it now at JonDavids.com/MarketingSuperpowers.

Or snap the QR code below:

SECTION 4

Communicating Your Message

CHAPTER 21

Learning to tell a story

My eyes are burning. My fingers won't move. Even if they did, I don't know where they would go. I've been staring at this screen for 38 minutes. I have nothing left to say. And it's clear that no one wants to hear me say it.

It's July 2021. I've been writing a post on LinkedIn every day for 7 months. Trying to grab some attention. Spread some value. Build an audience. Make a name for myself. But it feels more like I'm shouting into a tin can at the side of the freeway.

Seriously, no one cares.

I'm posting every day, getting barely 100 impressions. Maybe 1 or 2 likes. Pity likes.

Last week, a friend actually messaged me to ask if everything was alright. Why am I posting on LinkedIn so much? I'm too embarrassed to even explain.

I slam my laptop shut, lean back, and pick up a magazine beside me. Flipping through the pages, a story catches my eye. It's about a car wash. But it's not just any car wash. There are these guys who are buying old car washes, juicing them up, and turning them into big money-makers. It's a car wash rollup.

I finish the article and I'm still curious. So I start googling.

Two hours go by and I've learned so much about car washes. I figure other people might be interested too. I decide to flip open my laptop again.

And I start to write:

"I just heard about a company making almost $100M/yr selling car washes. I was blown away. So I spent 2 hours digging into the business. Here's what I learned."

I jot down the highlights point by point. Then I hit publish. Maybe this will get 4 likes? Maybe 9? Who knows. I shut my laptop and forget all about it.

Later that night I check back. And I can't believe what I see: 100 likes!

Whaaat? This is hard to process. But it feels great. I go to bed with a smile on my face.

The next morning I open LinkedIn and take another look. 350 likes. What the hell is going on?

By the end of that day it's 1,000. The next day it's 2,000. A day later it's 5,000.

And by the end of the week it's nearly 8,000 likes. Plus 100's of comments and shares.

But it gets better. I went from 0 followers to 10,000. Finally, I was learning to communicate a message.

If you enjoyed this, give me a follow and check out my podcast to hear how entrepreneurs are winning in all sorts of ways.

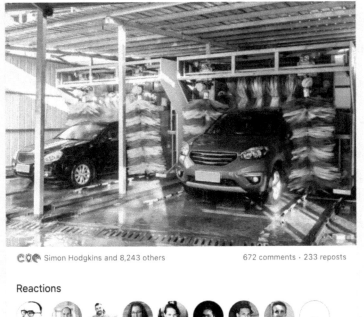

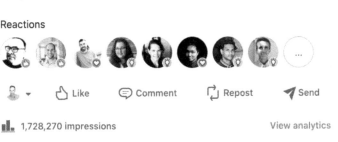

[Here's the car wash post. 1.7M impressions, 8,243 likes, 672 comments, and 233 reposts.]

You can read the car wash story on page 87. Or go to JonDavids.com/carwash.

I just heard about a company making almost $100M/yr selling car washes.

I was fascinated so I spent 2 hours digging into the business.

Here's what I learned:

The company is called Mammoth Holdings. They own nearly 100 car washes in places like Knoxville, Miami, and Utah Valley. And growing fast.

Mammoth is one of many firms that are rolling up car washes, with PE backing.

And it makes a lot of sense. Car washes can make $1M - $2.5M per year at a hefty profit. Especially if you know how to run them.

Here's the Mammoth playbook:

1/ Buy the biggest car wash in a small market

Mammoth doesn't actually build car washes. To enter a region, they acquire a popular brand with a few locations. This acts as their car wash platform for the market. They keep the name and continue picking off smaller players in that same market, rebranding them to match the platform. Before long, they are a dominant player.

2/ Implement a subscription model

This is the best part. Most of us pay for a car wash each time we go. But that can lead to a crummy business with spotty revenues. What happens when it rains and no one needs a wash? So Mammoth introduced a membership model. They charge $18 - $35 / month for unlimited washes. Each tier comes with its own perks like waxing and tire shining.

Get this – 60% of the company's revenue is recurring! This makes a lumpy revenue stream much more smooth and consistent.

3/ Put lots of automation in place

Once you get a car wash subscription, members get a radio-frequency identification tag to put in your windshield. The RFI tag tells the wash which package you have, chemicals are mixed automatically, and you drive right in. With this automation, a typical car wash can operate with just 2 employees. Huge boost to the bottom line.

4/ Acquire smart and finance well

Mammoth buys a mix of dominant car washes and smaller ones, paying higher and lower multiples for each, respectively. Then they will sell the real estate and rent it back from the new owner. This lets them pull out a chunk of capital asap. There's actually huge demand from real estate investors for the land that sits under car washes.

5/ Keep people and train them up

After an acquisition, Mammoth tries to retain existing employees. The company trains them on its playbook and promotes from within. This streamlines talent acquisition and keeps employees on board for much longer. You can go from working in a single car wash to managing an entire territory.

6/ Optimize back office functions

As you would expect, the company centralizes tasks like hiring, training, customer service, payroll and accounting. This lets them run an efficient operation and cuts down on redundant costs big time.

I'm sharing my car wash post for a specific reason. Yes, it's an example of content that reaches a lot of people. But there's a more important reason.

It's boring. Everything about it is boring. Car washes, business roll-ups, private equity, mergers and acquisitions, corporate strategy. Everything. There's nothing interesting here. At least, on the surface. And that's why it's such a good example. It shows that you can take something uninteresting and make it interesting.

Not only can you do this, but you must.

You make it interesting because of how you tell it, where you tell it, and who you tell it to.

If you want to communicate in a way that resonates with your buyer, you need to get good at making content. And then using that content to reinforce the main messages you want your target customer to believe in and remember.

In this section we'll cover two big topics on communicating your message: the "what" and the "how".

For the "what", there are 3 things we'll look at:

1. The purpose of your content.

2. The method of your content.

3. The form of your content

Afterwards, we'll cover the "how" with my best practices around copywriting, the basis of all great communication.

This section will build on itself and I can promise you, the skills you pick up will be insanely valuable.

So pay attention. Let's do it.

CHAPTER 22

The purpose of your content

The stuff you say needs to move people in some way. It should make them think. Or laugh. Or cry. Or wonder. Or learn. It can reinforce beliefs they already have. Or it can try to sway their beliefs with compelling arguments.

There are so many directions you can take it. But there's actually only 3 purposes a piece of content can have. It needs to do at least one of these 3 things:

1. Entertain

2. Educate

3. Inspire

Make sure you're doing one of these. Or two. Or all three. But never zero.

Entertainment

This category encompasses all the content we consume to escape from our everyday lives. It could be sports. Standup comedy. A drama on Netflix. A video on YouTube. A magic show. A rock concert. A talent competition. A cat dancing on Instagram. Literally anything that entertains you.

Something you watch where the payoff is just making you more happy, is entertainment.

Education

Now we're trying to learn stuff. It could be an online math course. A YouTube video on how to fix your car. A cooking class. A book on effective parenting. A tour guide.

Education is an enormous category, because it also includes the entire school system.

Colleges and universities, trade schools, elementary schools, advanced learning institutions, medical school, law school, career growth seminars, and so on.

People love to learn. And there's a class for everything.

Inspiration

The third bucket is inspiration. This is the stuff we watch and read to push ourselves forward. It reinforces the person we strive to be or the thing we want to become. It makes us feel strong and fulfilled.

Think of religious services. Self-help books. Tony Robbins. Oprah. Stories of overcoming turbulence, where the hero triumphs. Faith-based stories.

All these serve to inspire us. They provide the emotional and psychological energy to push forward and achieve our potential.

Add them up

Your content must serve at least one of these 3 purposes. But it's not limited to just one. In fact, lots of content is multi-purpose. A great Hollywood movie might entertain and inspire you. A mad scientist would educate and entertain you at the same time.

Maybe your college professor delivered a lesson that you found both educational and inspiring.

Having more than one purpose is fine. But it actually doesn't make the content better.

The most watched show on TV is NFL football. Are viewers inspired by the players? Maybe. Are they learning to play football? I doubt it. But are they entertained? You bet. That's why it's number one.

If you're in the finance industry and you go see the Chairman of the Federal Reserve speak at a conference, are you doing that to be entertained? Nope. Will you feel inspired? I doubt it. But you'll get a whole lot of educational value.

Choosing your content purpose

My bias is always towards entertainment alongside inspiration or education. There's just no excuse for someone creating content today and not trying to entertain. I think it's lazy. But more importantly, it's just bad business.

There is an exception though. If your content is incredibly exclusive and valuable, it can actually just be educational. If you run a hedge fund and decide to publish weekly videos of your stock picks along with spreadsheets detailing the analysis, I guarantee a lot of people would tune in. Not for the entertainment value, but for the education. And because they want to make money.

Take a look at your own strengths, those of your team, your brand, and the nature of what you're talking about. Based on those things, you should figure out your content purpose pretty quickly.

———

Now that you understand the 3 purposes that content can serve, here's the good news. The purpose of your content can change. You can educate on Monday, entertain on Thursday, and inspire on Sunday. You can mix it up all you want.

Just remember, you must always lean into at least one.

CHAPTER 23

The method of your content

There are 3 methods to making content. And no matter who you are or what your level of experience, you can definitely follow at least one of these methods.

They are:

1. Reporting

2. Documenting

3. Teaching

Let's look at each one in more detail.

Reporting

The most basic type of content creation is researching something and talking about it. This is called reporting. You can read a book, listen to a podcast, or just observe something in the wild. Then tell others.

Reporting can be surface level or incredibly detailed. I could read about a new way to barbecue chicken and make a TikTok telling you about it. Or I could investigate a major cybersecurity breach and write a 10-page white paper detailing the issues, the red flags, the people involved, and the fall out.

Both of these are examples of reporting.

You can create this type of content without any access or prior knowledge. The information is free and widely available. Podcasts, blogs, trade publications, newsletters, radio shows, YouTube channels. These are all places where you can learn stuff and tell others.

Of course, you can go deeper with first-hand interviews and in-depth investigations. But you don't need to. It's not required.

The great thing about reporting is that anyone can do it. If you're a total beginner with zero knowledge or experience, you can start reporting today. And you could do it for as long as you'd like. There are people who make content with the reporting method for their entire careers. They're called reporters!

I want to be clear here, I'm not suggesting that by reporting on a topic, you are a "reporter" in the formal or professional sense of the word. A reporter for the Wall Street Journal is clearly playing at a different level from the guy who listened to a podcast and then told his friends about it. I'm not trying to diminish the job of professional reporters. I'm simply using the word to describe this type of content creation.

If you're managing a new brand and if your main character doesn't have a ton of experience, I suggest reporting as the first method of generating content. Learn stuff and share along the way.

Documenting

If the main character is reporting on something that they are doing themselves, then it's actually called documenting. This is a step up from reporting because it requires that you are actually doing the work. And sharing your journey with others.

Documenting works well for people who are building something, learning a new skill, or going on an adventure. It can take on a different flavor from reporting because it's personal. You're the one doing it. And you're also the one sharing it. So it's personal from both angles.

The main character can document their journey by the minute, by the day, or by the week. They can share challenges, lessons, ups, downs, obstacles, victories, surprises, and more.

It builds more credibility for the character since they're not on the sidelines. They're in the arena. And it provides the consumer with a totally unique perspective. After all, anyone can report on public information. But you're the only one who can tell your own story.

And over time, all your documentation becomes proof that your opinions carry some weight. After all, you've lived it and shared the story in real time. Others will want to learn from you.

If your brand is in the building stage or the mature stage, documenting is a great place to start.

And there's one more method of content creation.

Teaching

Teaching is the hardest thing to do. And it's not because you're a bad teacher. You might be a great teacher. But if you, as the main character, don't already have a public image, you have zero credibility. No one will care about what you have to say.

By public image, I mean that people have to know you. Maybe you've been posting on social media for a long time, or writing a blog, or publishing a newsletter, or appearing on TV. You might have years of experience doing amazing things, but if you've been doing it in the dark, you have no public image.

That's why this one is last. Because it's so tempting. Everyone thinks they can start with teaching. They can't.

I know it's harsh but 95% of the people putting out "educational" content should not be. And then they wonder why their content doesn't perform. Why no one is watching. After all, other people put out similar content and they get 10,000 likes. But you only get 2 likes. And one is your mom. Why is that?

I'll tell you exactly why that is:

Because learning is more about the person, and less about the information.

I would love to learn music from Beethoven. Science from Einstein. Art from Picasso. Software from Bill Gates. Investing from Warren Buffett.

Is it because these people are the best in the world at those things? That's part of it. But also because they're famous.

I'm sure there are scholars at the greatest universities who can teach those subjects as well or better than these people. But I'd still rather learn from these people. Right or wrong. It doesn't matter. And I'm sure lots of others would too.

It's human nature. We want to learn from people who have demonstrated their own abilities. So you need to demonstrate your abilities before anyone else is going to care.

What's that? You're already an expert? Oh okay.

Let's say you have lots of experience. Maybe you've earned a business degree and worked as a senior executive at a Fortune 500 company. You have 15 years experience at the highest levels of finance or manufacturing or technology. You can definitely jump straight to teaching, right?

Wrong.

Again, you haven't earned the public credibility. Not yet anyway.

First, you must document.

Think about it. Our main character might have lots of experience. They might have credentials. They might have wisdom. But no one knows that. We haven't lived their life. There's no camera sitting at the side of their desk broadcasting their daily experience to the world. They need to build credibility first. Before they can teach us anything. And to build credibility, they must document.

Tell us about their history, their learnings, tough lessons, biggest wins and hard losses. Take us into their experiences. So it feels like we're living vicariously through them. Do this for a few months or a year. Earn our respect. And then teach us.

And if the main character doesn't have much personal experience, that's fine too.

When a celebrity or influencer takes on the role of the main character, they often never teach. Instead they act as the voice of the customer. Asking questions and reporting on the answers. Or documenting their own experiences as they learn.

Teaching always comes last. After reporting and documenting you will have trust. And people will beg for you to teach them.

———

Choosing your content method

For any new brand where the founder is the main character, the content method will likely follow the sequence of reporting, then documenting, then teaching. Establish yourself in one, then move to the next.

If you are already building or doing something, you can skip reporting and start at documenting.

But unless you already have a public image, you must document first.

For growing or mature brands, choose the content method that makes sense for your main character.

As you move forward, you can always move backwards too. You can also combine more than one method in your content. You can document and teach. You can report and document. You can teach and report.

Over time, you'll find your flow.

CHAPTER 24

The form of your content

Now you're getting a feel for your purpose and your method. Next you need a way to tell these stories. You need to choose a form.

There are 4 content forms to choose from:

1. Written content

2. Visual content

3. Audio content

4. Audio/visual content

We'll look at each one in more detail now.

Written content

This is the most primal form of mass communication. And still incredibly effective.

A piece of written content could be a blog or a LinkedIn post. It could be short form like a post on X. Or it could be long form like an essay.

Many people deeply undervalue the power of the written word. And that's because they don't know how to write. They learned how to write in school. Essays and reports. That's good for academic stuff. But it's not actually great writing.

You see, great writing pulls you in like a magnet. It's irresistible. A slippery slope that hooks your reader from the first sentence and fills their mind with curiosity and suspense. So they simply can't look away.

The best copywriting will drive massive attention and generate millions in revenue.

I know this because I do it every day. And I'll show you how it's done in just a little bit.

Visual content

For the purpose of this discussion, visual content is any picture without sound. Think about a classic Instagram post. But it can be a lot more than that. It's a meme. Or a gif. It's a photo with text on top. It's a cartoon with your face superimposed on it.

You can do amazing storytelling with nothing but visual content. A great example of this is the Instagram channel Humans of New York. To be fair, that channel also has written content, with the long caption on each photo. But the photos themselves tell a story.

Another is Litquidity. This started as an X account posting memes about the world of finance. The content has evolved since then, but this meme-lord still reigns supreme.

Audio content

The world of audio has had a full resurgence. Commercial radio was revolutionary when it was invented in 1920. And now a century later it's on a tear again.

But this time it's different. Modern audio content is on-demand, hyper-niche, and freely available to anyone, anywhere. As long as they have an internet connection. That's why we've seen the explosive growth of podcasts. This is one of my favorite mediums for a few reasons.

A podcast gives you a direct connection to your audience. No algorithm or platform can shut you down.

Listeners subscribe directly to your podcast via an app like Apple Podcasts or Spotify. And once they subscribe, new episodes are pushed directly to their phone or computer.

Podcasts also have a very high retention rate, meaning most people tune in for most or all of an episode. And they won't be consuming a whole bunch of other stuff at the same time. Unlike watching a video or reading a blog, it's hard to get distracted with other audio. Our ears can really only tune in to one thing at a time, while our eyes can take in a whole bunch at once. This splinters our attention. That doesn't happen with podcasts.

But of course, there is a downside. Podcasts are an island. It's hard for people to find your podcast unless you already have an audience. There's no recommendation engine or built-in sharing tool. If I see an Instagram post and hit the like button, the post will show up for some of the people that follow me. When this happens over and over, lots of people see it. But nothing like this exists in the world of podcasts.

So I recommend starting with something else – say a newsletter, Instagram, or YouTube. Build an audience first and then launch your podcast. Not to say you can't do both at once. But if you're constrained by resources, podcasts are usually a tough place to start.

Audio/visual content

Video is the closest thing we have to a real life interaction, on an infinite scale. People can see your face. Look into your eyes. Observe your body language. Feel like you're speaking directly to them.

You can add in graphics, sounds, animations, smash cuts, and an endless number of other effects to punch up your story.

Videos can also be cartoons or animations. It can be a voiceover with imagery rolling on screen. Think of a voice talking about their childhood, and on screen you see images and video of kids playing.

You can also just have words on screen with music in the background. These were super popular in the 1990's. They were called "video sales letters" or VSL's. Today a VSL refers to anyone making a sales pitch in a video. But now you know where the term came from.

Choosing your content form

Picking your form comes down to 3 things:

- Your preference

- Market preference

- Platform preference

1. Your preference

Depending on the main character's personality, they will probably be drawn to one form over another. Maybe you're a wordsmith. Or maybe you're a talker. Or maybe you like crafting beautiful photos. Perhaps you light up in front of the camera. Whichever is most natural for the character will probably end up producing the highest quality content.

2. Market preference

Certain categories of content lean towards one form over another. If you're trying to entertain people with a science experiment, the consumer would likely prefer video over a written piece.

If you were showing the before/after transformation of a weight loss journey, people would expect a photo.

Sometimes, it's less obvious. I could deliver all the information I'm giving you now in written form (this book), audio form (an audio recording of the book), or through a video (like a course). I've actually done all 3 because there's a market for each. I'm also making short form content using the snippets from this book on multiple platforms.

It's ideal to give the consumer choice, and allow them to pick their form. But if you have limited time and resources, pick the one that fits the largest portion of the market.

3. Platform preference

Depending on what platform you choose, the delivery method could be determined for you. Even platforms that allow multiple delivery options, bias towards certain ones.

For example, LinkedIn allows videos. But I've found videos never perform as well as written content. X is the same.

Instagram favored photos for a long time. Then videos took over with Instagram Reels.

YouTube has long form videos and short form videos. And they drive attention to these formats in different ways.

Leaning into the platform allows you to optimize for reach.

———

I recommend starting with your preference, then market preference, then platform preference. I say this because you or your main character or your team actually needs to make content everyday for a very long time. So you need to enjoy it. Your preference comes first.

If you enjoy making the content and you're getting better at it every day, your market will naturally like it too. And if you can draw in an audience, the platforms will surface your content.

Ultimately, you will use every form on every platform. That's the path of all successful brands. It's just good business. So you really just need to worry about getting started. The rest will take care of itself.

CHAPTER 25

Getting your message in front of the right people

There are 2 ways to communicate with your market:

1. Organic - The term "organic" refers to all the "free" channels, like your social media, podcast, email, website, blogs, and doing interviews with media outlets. We think of these as "free" because you're not paying anyone to distribute your message for you. Collectively, we call these "organic channels".

2. Paid - This refers to all the channels you must pay for. Things like advertising on Facebook or TikTok, buying ads on Google, paying for commercial time on the radio or podcasts, renting a billboard at the side of the highway, sponsoring an event, and so on. In these cases, you are paying others to distribute your message. So we call them "paid channels".

Let's look at each one more closely.

Organic Channels

Depending on what study you're reading, anywhere from 50% to 80% of consumers discover brands and products organically on social media. The numbers are high across other organic channels too, like podcasts and blogs.

Your customers and potential customers can engage with you through comments, likes, emails, direct messages, or by sharing the content with others. And of course, they can reach out to buy your product or service.

The limitation with your organic channels is that people need to find them. You can write a blog post with helpful advice for massage therapists, but there's no guarantee that a massage therapist will read it.

Because of this, it's even more important that your organic content is interesting and that you are consistent with it. As people discover it and share it with friends, they'll come back for more. And if you're not delivering, they'll go somewhere else.

Not all organic channels are created equal. Podcasts, blogs, and websites require people to find you in places they don't normally go. After all, no one is punching your website address into their browser if they've never heard of you. It's kind of like you're on a deserted island and you're hoping a boat or airplane will come by and find you. It could happen, but it's a longshot.

On the other hand, social channels, like Instagram, LinkedIn, and YouTube make it easy for strangers to find your content. When someone likes, comments, or shares content on these platforms, it's automatically exposed to a wider audience. This is kind of like standing in front of a crowd. Even if no one knows who you are, there's a chance you can grab attention if you've got an interesting message.

For all these reasons, I suggest a mix of organic channels. Some like an island and some like a crowd.

Paid Channels

When you need to get your message to a specific person, in a specific place, at a specific time, paid channels are the way to go. And when you put your message onto a paid channel, people stop referring to it as "content" and start referring to it as an "advertisement".

This is a big mistake. Because it makes you lazy and complacent. Just think about that word: "ad". It conjures up the idea of an interruption. If you grew up watching TV in the 90's, the commercials were a time to get up and use the bathroom. And if you're watching YouTube today, an ad is that thing playing on screen while you watch the countdown clock in the bottom right corner.

5-4-3-2-1. Skip Ad.

How fast can you click it? I'm at about 1/10th of a second.

Let's face it, with the exception of the Super Bowl and a few of your favorite brands, no one wants to watch an ad. And because I feel so strongly about this, I'm not going to use the word "ad". I'm going to say content. Because that's what it is. The best content you can possibly make, that you happen to put on paid channels.

Think of a paid channel like renting real estate. But instead of renting a house to live in or an office to work in, you're renting space in someone's eyes or ears.

This has several benefits. You can rent this real estate wherever you want, whenever you want, and as much as you want.

For example, if I want to reach pharmaceutical executives who work in Zurich for 3 weeks in the month of May, I can do that. I can buy advertising space on a big site like LinkedIn, which will target that specific market. Or I can go much more niche and advertise in a trade magazine that specifically caters to pharmaceutical executives in Zurich.

Extremely powerful, as you can see.

But there are downsides to paid channels too. The big one is that you are forcing people to view your content. They're not seeking it out, no one has referred them to it, and they might not have time for it.

Nevertheless, when done right it definitely works. It all comes down to the strength of the content.

There are entire books and courses on how to use paid channels. For the purposes of this book, I just want you to understand that it is one place you can distribute your content. And now you know why you might want to do that.

CHAPTER 26

The right message at the right time

Now that we have a sense of what, where, and when to communicate, we can start meshing these concepts. For example, say thing A, to group B, at time C. Or say thing B, to group C, at time A. Or say thing C, to group A, at time B.

Get the idea? This part is actually more simple than it sounds. All thanks to 3 tasty acronyms:

1. ToFU

2. MoFU

3. BoFU

These stand for:

1. Top of Funnel

2. Middle of Funnel

3. Bottom of Funnel

Let me explain how funnels work.

I want you to picture a pyramid. Now flip it upside down so the widest part is at the top and the little pointy part is on the bottom. Now imagine customers are standing on top of your upside down pyramid. They're standing there because you've created something that grabbed their attention. These are brand new people, who may never have heard of you. They don't know who you are, or what you do, or who you do it for, or if you're any good at doing that thing.

They just heard of you and decided to give you 5 seconds of their brain power.

These people are at the top of your funnel or "ToFU" for short. When potential customers are at the ToFU, you should speak to them at a very high level. You wouldn't drop the name of your product because they won't know what you're talking about. And they might be turned off feeling like they're being sold to.

You also can't assume people who are at the ToFU are really a part of your movement yet. They could just be silent spectators.

But let's assume these people move down the imaginary pyramid. Now they're in the middle of the funnel or "MoFU". At this point, they could be resonating with what you're saying and showing some level of interest. You have staying power in their mind. Plus, now that they're getting to know you better, you can go deeper into references that a total newbie wouldn't understand.

And now let's say they go straight to the bottom. This is called bottom of funnel or "BoFU". At this point, they're definitely fans and believers of what you say and do. These people are the most likely to become your customers.

What I just described is called a marketing funnel. And every customer goes through it at their own speed. They become aware of you at the ToFU. They start to know, like, and trust you in the MoFU. And they buy from you at the BoFU.

The marketing funnel connects back to the Movement Formula in an important way. Do you see it?

Don't worry – I'll tell you.

ToFU → Unifying belief

MoFU → Faith

BoFU → Action

At the ToFU, you drive your unifying belief in all sorts of creative ways. Telling stories, asking questions, sharing bumper sticker sayings.

At the MoFU, you are driving faith in unique and interesting ways. Testimonials, case studies, and stories of transformation.

At the BoFU, you are making it easy for people to take action. Buy my product, buy my product, buy my product.

If you build it right, your Movement Formula will push people through the funnel like a slip 'n slide. It's a beautiful thing.

CHAPTER 27

The 7 Ground Rules of Copywriting

Now that we've covered the "what" of communicating your message, let's move on to the "how". I believe copywriting is the basis for strong communication, whether it's written or spoken. Copywriting is the practice of writing specifically for marketing purposes. Think of headlines, billboards, and sales letters.

What that really means is it has to be top-notch writing. The kind of writing that grabs you by the collar and puts you in a bear hug. Copywriting is about using your words like magnets.

If you're writing content, then obviously copywriting is important. It's the very essence of what you're doing. And if you're speaking, the words you say will be based on a script or format that echoes the principles of copywriting. Even if you're talented enough to improvise what you say, you'll follow copywriting principles if you want to be memorable.

First we'll cover my 7 essential ground rules for copywriting. The lessons in these next chapters will help you to write your origin story, blogs, social media posts, website text, video scripts, sales letters, and more.

And I'll have even additional resources at the end of this section.

Buckle up big rig. Let's make your words sing.

CHAPTER 28

Grade 3 language

For your copywriting to be effective, people need to easily understand it. And to understand it, your words should be simple. People who use big words are usually trying to sound smart. People who are actually smart know how to explain complicated things so anyone can understand.

It's kind of like watching an NBA player on the court. Do they make basketball look hard? Are they straining to dunk? Pulling a muscle on a chest pass? No. It's the opposite. They make it look way too easy. That's why it's fun to watch.

It's the same with your language. It doesn't matter how complicated the subject is. People will only consume and enjoy it, if they understand it.

For example, here are two versions of the same sentence. Which is going to get more attention?

Version #1:

If you're subject to frequent abdominal pains, this new medication could be the appropriate remedy.

Version #2:

Stomachache? Take this medicine. You'll feel better fast.

They both mean the same thing. But clearly version 2 is simpler than version 1.

When in doubt, always go simple.

If you need some help with this, use an AI tool to simplify your language. Just paste your sentence into an AI language app, and type "rewrite this at a grade 3 level". Then modify it to ensure it's in the right tone and voice. Before long, you'll be doing it with no help at all.

CHAPTER 29

Tailor Your Lingo to Your Reader

Experts sometimes don't realize when they're using terms no one understands but them. And lingo is actually a strong signal of the buyer you are targeting.

If you're trying to attract people who are advanced in a particular field, lingo is an effective filter. It's like a dog whistle. It's a wink to the reader that this is for you. It also shuts out amateurs because they have no idea what you're talking about.

But this also works in reverse. If you're trying to target a customer who is not an expert in your field, don't use insider lingo.

For example, let's say I sell auto parts for race cars. I could say something like this:

Version #1:

When your car hits 200mph, the downforce is fierce.

A racing enthusiast knows what "downforce" means. But what if I'm targeting non-experts. I can't just drop that word because they won't know what it means. I would need to clearly explain my lingo. So I could say something like this:

Version #2:

Imagine you're in a race car and there's this huge hand pushing down on your hood while you circle the track. We call that downforce. And it keeps your car stuck to the ground like glue. Even if you're driving at 200mph.

Anyone can understand version #2. So you've expanded your universe of interested readers.

Remember, lingo is a filter. Use it wisely.

CHAPTER 30

Economy of words

There are lots of words that simply don't need to be there. One common reason is the use of adjectives to make up for weak verbs. Here's an example:

Version #1:

She closed the door really hard.

Do you see the unnecessary word? "Really" doesn't need to be there. It's acting as a crutch for a weak verb: "hard". Let's try this instead:

Version #2:

She slammed the door.

See that? We eliminated 33% of the words and strengthened the sentence. "Closed really hard" means the same thing as "slammed".

Fewer words, bigger impact. I love it.

The other place writers get too wordy is with filler words. Take this example:

Version #1:

She told him that he needed to be there by 5pm.

I'm spotting three words that are bloating this sentence. It's a total waste of space.

Here's my fix:

Version #2:

She told him to be there by 5pm.

Those three clunky words — *that he needed* — are a waste of space. And while these might seem like tiny details, I assure you they're not. You're sucking up your reader's valuable time for no reason.

If you asked me for the best route to the airport, the implication is that you want the "fastest" route to the airport. Avoid traffic, construction, and potholes. Your copywriting is the same. Readers want the most direct route. So put them in the express lane.

Challenge yourself to say more with less words. Get rid of those bumps. And you'll start seeing a lot more traffic. (The good kind).

CHAPTER 31

Paint a Picture

Great copywriting isn't boring. It's descriptive. It's imaginative. The reader should feel like they're being transported to a different time and place. The words are your paintbrush and the empty page is your canvas.

Let's say I'm trying to appeal to people who are on the fence with running a digital marketing program. I could say this:

Version #1:

Are you having difficulty with your digital marketing? Online advertising can be quite challenging and business owners often struggle with this tactic. But you're not alone and we can help you achieve great results!

Are you asleep yet? Because I almost passed out while writing that.

There's no emotion in it. I didn't get under the reader's skin. I'm not inside their head. I need to dig deeper. What is the reader feeling? What keeps them up at night? What makes them smile? What gives them heartburn?

Let's channel our inner Leonardo da Vinci and try that again:

Version #2:

I know what you're thinking. Should I be running Facebook ads? I'm getting 100 clicks but no one's buying. Literally zero sales. Just lighting my cash on fire. And I'm not even ranking on Google! I think I'm on page 9. Who visits page

9? I hired an SEO guy 8 months ago and he tells me it's working. Am I paying for fairy dust?

Notice how version 2 goes into the mind of the buyer. As though we're reading their thoughts. And that's the point.

If you're targeting a specific persona, you need to get into their head. Make it feel like you're speaking directly to them.

The page is your canvas. Paint something with impact.

CHAPTER 32

Start with action

You know those action movies that start smack in the middle of a heist? They pull you in from the first beat. They capture your attention and curiosity. Then keep you glued to the screen. Before you know it, 2 hours have passed and the credits are rolling.

Those movies start with action. And that's a common tactic in strong copywriting. Because there's no time to waste. A reader will decide to stick with you or bail after just a few sentences. If you're lucky.

The mistake people make is they begin at the beginning. Probably because those words sound the same. But that's a huge mistake. You need to begin at the *point of high action*.

Here's an example:

I sat up, looked to my left, and then I saw it.

Coming at me like a freight train. I knew I had to stop it, before she found out.

What was I looking at?

It all started 4 hours earlier.

You don't even know what I'm talking about, but I'll bet you're curious. Right?

What's on your left? What do you see? What happened 4 hours earlier? Who is "she"?

Oh, I bet you'd like to know.

Well, the answer is nothing. I'm just grabbing your attention.

And it worked.

CHAPTER 33

Emotion first, logic second

People make decisions with their hearts and reinforce those decisions with their heads. We do it all the time. You feel the emotional pull and then your head jumps in, convincing you why this is the right decision.

There are other influence factors too, but this order usually doesn't change. And that means emotion is just as important as logic. Maybe more.

You can use this in your copywriting by targeting the feeling first and the facts second. Here's a piece of writing to show you what I mean. As you read it, see if you can pinpoint whether I'm appealing to your heart or your head.

Sample Writing:

I remember what things were like before I joined the gym. It sucked. I felt crummy looking in the mirror. I would run out of breath just walking up the stairs. Cracking a sweat strolling from the car to my front door. And I knew I wasn't giving my body the attention it deserved. I'm better than this.

So I decided to make a change. To take real action and get my life back on track. I joined Sanctuary Gym. And I'm so glad I did. It's close to my house, my friends are there every morning, and the price is right.

If you look at these two paragraphs, you'll notice the first one is all about the feeling. Anyone who struggles with their body image can relate to some of those feelings. I'm appealing to your emotion.

In the second paragraph, I'm touching on the facts. Distance, familiar faces, and the right price. These are logical considerations that are important to your decision.

This is a powerful 1-2 punch. Pull at the heartstrings then make sense of it in the brain.

CHAPTER 34

Polarization is Good

Want to be liked by everyone?

Too bad. If you want some people to love you, it's important to accept that some people aren't going to like you at all. How could it go any other way?

If your writing is any good, it likely takes a stand. You are *for* one thing and *against* something else.

The people who are for the same thing as you, will love it. Those who are against it, will not.

And with any luck, they'll voice their displeasure. You can think of these people as your critics. But I call them "haters".

Haters are a powerful tool for community building. Because they empower the lovers to speak up.

Everyone digs into their positions. And becomes more passionate about those opinions.

In some categories, it goes deeper than just an opinion. It's self identity. It's status. It's a part of who you are. And that means something.

To show you the power of polarization, here are a few pieces of content I created that blew up because of all the hate they got.

I wrote about my 17-year-old neighbor who was earning $4,200/month from his side hustle. It was seen by over 1 million people and received 6,000 likes and comments. Some of those comments were celebrating his success. And some of them were throwing stones.

 Jon Davids · You
CEO of Influicity. Turn your marketing into a superpower....
11mo · 🌐

My 17-year-old neighbour is making $4,200/mth from his side hustle.

And it takes him 3 hours a week....   ...see more

👍❤️ 5,476   460 comments · 108 reposts

 Like   Comment   Repost   Send

This was a polarizing post

This kid is a scam artist. This kid is a thief. This story is made up.

That was just some of what I saw.

Well, it's a true story. And it's not even that hard to believe in my opinion. Check out the difference in these two comments.

Lovers

Kid's a genius - I realized that when I saw his target market: 65+. They not only have the money to spend, they DON'T want to mess with trying to fix technical gadgets themselves. He can also branch out into taking on small DIY projects around the home and make a small fortune there, too.

Haters

Hustler is right. Exploiting elderly people by selling them a support package they don't need and won't use. I hope they have financial advisors who will question what they are getting for their $1,188 per year.

Like ❤️😊 27   Reply 7

You see how strong people are in their beliefs? How they identify so firmly with them? And how vocal they are about it?

All that polarization lifted this post up and made it memorable. More importantly, it amplified the reach tremendously. I got thousands of new followers and email subscribers.

This is strong copywriting at work.

You can read the post about my 17-year-old neighbor on page 130. Or go to JonDavids.com/neighbor.

———

My 17-year-old neighbor is making $4,200/mth from his side hustle.

And it takes him 3 hours a week.

I think it's freakin' awesome, so I'm gonna tell you about it.

- the hustler is Cooper, a tech-savvy teenager
- the business is a "neighborhood Geek Squad"

1/ How it works

On-call tech support for everything around your home, like setting up a new modem or figuring out why your Sonos stopped working.

2/ Who it's for

Targeting an older demo of 65+. They have money to spend and gadgets to fix.

3/ The revenue model

It's $99/mth all-in and he currently has 42 clients. There are some parameters around what is and isn't included. But I don't know the details.

4/ How he runs it

It's just him and occasionally a buddy helping him out. Customers can call, text, or email and he mostly works evenings, 6p-9p. Typically makes 4 house calls a week.

5/ What do I think

This hustle's so hot I gotta crank up my A/C.

First off, he had me at recurring revenue. My heart skipped a beat.

Second, it's flexible. Set your own hours, choose a max number of clients, and create the ground rules for servicing.

Third, it works for a teenager with a few hours a week or a professional working a full time job.

Plus, there are a TON of ways to grow and improve this simple business. Here are a few:

→ expand to more areas and customers

→ outsource the labor to other locals

→ generate demand with SEM, flyers, direct mail

→ increase prices with tiered packages

→ add appliance-care

→ up-sell related products like gadgets and software

→ offer full set-up & installation for home theaters, etc.

The list goes on.

Young Cooper will do just fine.

Here's another piece of content. In this one, I'm talking about a popular cookie business. Again, some people love these cookies and some people hate them.

Look at this comment:

It's a pretty amazing brand story considering the cookies are forgettable at best.

Like 💬 29   Reply 7

This simple, sarcastic comment received 29 reactions and 7 replies. One person throws shade at the cookies and a bunch of others jump on the bandwagon.

I see this all the time. And it's great for virality. Don't shy away from polarization.

———

Let's do a quick recap of the 7 copywriting ground rules.

1. Grade 3 language

2. Tailor your lingo to the reader

3. Economy of words

4. Paint a picture

5. Start with action

6. Emotion first, logic second

7. Polarization is good

Now let's bring those rules to life with the essential copywriting template: AIDA.

CHAPTER 35

An intro to AIDA

AIDA is an acronym for:

Attention

Interest

Desire

Action

The AIDA method was developed by Elias St. Elmo Lewis, an American advertising professional. He came up with AIDA as a marketing model, back in 1898. He realized that customers go through a series of steps when making purchasing decisions.

Turns out he was right. And it formed the basis of all good copywriting over the last century.

You can't understand copywriting without understanding AIDA.

CHAPTER 36

Attention

The very first thing your writing must do is get the attention of the reader. It's so obvious, right? Yes. But it's not intuitive.

Like I said in copywriting ground rule #4, our natural instinct is to begin writing from the beginning. How does the thing we're talking about start? But that's usually not when your copywriting starts. Because it's the least interesting part.

How does a hurricane start? With complete stillness.

Snoozeville.

We need to start with action. Adventure. Curiosity. Suspense. Drama. Or at least the perception that one of those things is about to happen.

When I tell my origin story of how I became an entrepreneur, I start with this line: "I built an internet company in college making $300K/year. And I didn't know anything about the internet. Let me tell you exactly how I did it."

Suppose that instead, I started the story with:

"I needed money in college. And it was hard getting a job. So I started researching how I could make money…"

That's a one-way ticket to yawn city.

Do you see how important it is to get attention at the very start? Especially in a world where the competition for attention is ferocious. People are anxious to jump to the next thing. So give them a reason to stick with you.

Here are 3 ways to grab attention:

1. Start with the payoff

Begin with the climax of the story. What's the big win coming at the end? Put it at the front. You might think this ruins the story, but it doesn't need to.

We all know the ship sank at the end of Titanic. But that movie still made $2 billion. Because the movie wasn't actually about a sinking ship. It was about a love story. And my origin story is not about the $300,000. It's about how I earned that money.

It's easy to start with the payoff when readers already know the ending. But if you prefer not to reveal the ending, you can phrase it as a tease. Staying with the example of my origin story, instead of saying:

Version #1:

"I built an internet company in college making $300K/year."

I could say this instead:

Version #2:

"I had one goal in college: to make $300,000. Here's what happened next."

In the second version, I'm not actually revealing that I made $300,000. Only that this was my goal. And the reader can find out whether I succeeded by reading the story.

In both versions, I'm leading with the payoff. But I'm evoking curiosity in version #2.

Which leads to my next attention grabber.

2. Evoke Curiosity

You need to make them wonder. What are you talking about? What does that sentence mean? How could you possibly say that? How did that even work?

These are all questions your reader should be asking.

To evoke curiosity, look for juxtaposed information. Things that don't make sense together. If I just said "I made $300,000" and left it there, you probably wouldn't be so curious. But throwing in that I earned this money in college kicks it up a notch.

I call this juxtaposed information. College students aren't supposed to earn $300,000. If anything, they're supposed to be in debt by $300,000. (Unfortunately).

I also said that I made that money by starting an internet company, and I didn't know anything about the internet. Again, I'm layering on more juxtaposed information. After all, how does someone build a business in an area they know nothing about?

No matter what you're discussing, there's usually a thread of juxtaposed information. Tug at it.

- The 4-year-old who is also a math genius

- The dog who does yoga

- The plumber who made $11 million last year

These things don't need to be 100% true. You can temper your words later and explain what you really meant. But use them to craft an enticing headline. Seek out 2 things that don't make total sense when you put them together. That's how you evoke curiosity.

3. Be relatable or aspirational – but not untouchable

You need to connect with the reader in order to grab their attention. And to do that, they must relate to what you're saying. If they can't relate right now, they should aspire to relate.

But if you go too far, it becomes untouchable.

At Influicity, we manage social media accounts for lots of clients. A little while ago, we wrote a story that was posted to LinkedIn. The opening line went something like this:

"Angela built a $2 billion company with one key insight…"

The post performed okay. But we thought it could do better. So we kept thinking.

This particular entrepreneur did have a business that was valued at $2 billion. But that number was untouchable for a lot of the target audience. We needed to go lower. So we modified it to:

"Angela paid herself $14 million last year by figuring out one thing…"

Both statements are true. Angela's company was valued at $2 billion based on a recent round of funding. And she also paid herself $14 million in a secondary financing. (That's when an early shareholder gets to take cash off the table during a funding round.)

So in this case, we just cherry-picked a different piece of the story and used it as our opening. As it turns out, the $14 million number was more relatable or aspirational for the target audience of this particular client.

The second version performed much better.

————

As an example, I'm going write an opening line that will grab the reader's attention:

Attention: I just bought a private jet for $32

Interest:

Desire:

Action:

Did that get your attention? I hope so. I'm starting with the payoff - the fact that I just bought a private jet. I'm also evoking curiosity with juxtaposed information. After all, how can a private jet cost $32? And it's just a little bit aspirational. There are many people who want to buy a private jet. Especially with that price tag.

In this example, I'm using all of the methods I just described to grab attention. But you obviously don't need to do that. I'm just trying to illustrate how you could do it.

Now that I have your attention, it's time to create some interest.

CHAPTER 37

Interest

You've captured attention for a moment. That's the job of your first line. But the real job of your first line is to get people to read the second line. And the job of the second line is to get people reading the third line. You get the idea.

It's time to pique the reader's interest. Here are 3 ways I like to approach the Interest step.

1. How does it affect the reader?

I want you to answer one simple question: "what's in it for me?"

That's exactly what your reader is going to be asking. And you better tell them fast. Can they benefit from the thing that just caught their attention? Can they use it to get something they want? Or avoid something they hate? Does it solve a burning problem that's been bugging them for months? Will it answer a vexing question that's bouncing around their brain?

This is a very personal experience. Your reader is selfish. As they should be. You've sucked them into a vortex of words and all they want is a reason to leave. Don't let them. Use this moment to make it all about them. And kick their interest into high gear.

2. Enhance the pleasure / twist the knife

If your opening line was about a good thing, you may pique the reader's interest by making that good thing even better. You've just handed them an ice cream sundae. Now drizzle on some chocolate sauce, a swirl of whipped cream, and a maraschino cherry.

As an example, let's say my opening line is: "Maddy's Furniture is having a 50% off blowout sale this weekend". Then my interest grabber might be: "And the first 100 shoppers get a free gift worth $250."

I was already interested in the cheap furniture and now you're making the good thing even better with a free gift.

But what if it's not a good thing? What if you've just delivered a very bad thing? Well then, it's time to twist the knife. Make it worse. You just gave them a papercut. Now grab a fistful of salt and start rubbing it in. Let's get that cut burning.

For example, let's say my opening line is:

"Your taxes are going to increase by 12% next year."

Then my interest grabber might be:

"And if you don't file this form in the next 24 hours, that number will double."

Make the good thing better or make the bad thing worse. These are strong interest grabbers.

3. Compound the confusion

If your attention grabber created some confusion, then your interest line could simply compound that confusion. You already have them wondering, so let's keep them wondering.

In this case, maybe you opened with a line like: "I haven't had any water in 9 days."

I'm already confused because I didn't think a human could go that long without water. So my interest grabber might be:

"And my doctor tells me this is actually the best thing I can do for my body."

Okay, now I'm super confused. You haven't drank any water and there's a doctor telling you this is a good thing? That it's actually beneficial? You definitely have my interest.

Side note: You definitely need to drink water daily. Please don't take this silly copywriting example as health advice.

————————

Going back to our running example, let's add in some interest:

Attention: I just bought a private jet for $32

Interest: And you can get one right now for only $28

Desire:

Action:

See what I did there? Again, I'm using all 3 methods to really make it clear.

First, I'm answering the big question - *what's in it for me*. I'm telling you that you can also get a private jet. You were probably a little jealous that I bought one. So being able to get one yourself immediately scratches that itch.

I'm also making the good thing better. You might have been a little happy for me since I got a private jet. Or maybe not! But I think we can agree that getting one yourself is way better.

Finally, I'm compounding the confusion by throwing in an even more absurd price. Mine was $32 but you can get yours for just $28. What?! Where are these dirt cheap private jets coming from? This sounds insane.

It's supposed to. I want you to read the next line, remember?

Okay, so I've grabbed your attention and hooked your interest. Time to lay it on thick by creating serious desire.

CHAPTER 38

Desire

I got a serious lesson in desire a few years ago in New York City.

I'm wrapping up a day of client meetings, walking through Times Square. The time is around 6pm. I pass by a row of restaurants. Busy places that get a lot of tourist traffic, I'm sure.

Outside each one is a well-dressed man or a woman. They're all smiling and saying things like: "we have an open table!" or "come in and try the pasta of the day!" Each restaurant I pass, someone is telling me to come in and eat. Why are these people so eager to feed me?

It's their job, of course. They want to get foot traffic in the door. And my feet are as good as anyone else's.

One of these people catches my attention. So I glance inside the window of the restaurant. Is it full? Yup, there are a few people inside. And I see a few others grabbing a table right now.

I turn to my colleague. "Are you hungry?"

"I could be," he replies.

I glance down at a large menu on a little podium, browsing the dishes. The well-dressed man leans in and says he can seat us right away. He goes on about the chef's signature dishes and the drink specials.

Let's pause here. What's happening exactly?

The well-dressed man is getting my attention. The people enjoying their meals inside the restaurant are piquing my interest. Now I'm glancing at the menu. And the well-dressed man is talking up the tastiness.

This is called desire. And if this restaurant is any good, that desire should be flooding through me.

In copywriting, this piece is the glue. We've already seized the attention and spiked the interest. Now it's time to make it worthwhile.

Here are 3 ways to bring out desire:

1. Time Travel

As the writer, you must have a sense of how you felt before and after you heard or experienced the thing you're talking about. What was that like? It's important to really think this through. Because the more clear this picture is in your mind, the more clearly you can explain it to your reader.

Think of this like time travel. What pleasure or pain would your reader be feeling moments *before* the thing you're talking about? How will that change afterwards?

To jumpstart your writing, use phrases like:

"Imagine if you had this right now..."

or

"Wouldn't it be cool if…"

or

"If I gave you this, do you think you could…"

We're really trying to emphasize the thing we're talking about. Bring it to life. In technicolor. Take your reader to that place in their mind where this has already happened. Let them experience it through your words.

2. Get Specific

Now is the time to sweat the details. Get into the weeds. Be intentional with your words and phrases.

Are you talking about a dog? Or a white dog? Or a tiny, white dog? Or a tiny, white dog wearing a blue collar? Or a tiny, white dog wearing a blue collar, being carried around in a $4,000 purse?

I know exactly what kind of dog you're picturing right now. We all do. Because I'm being very specific.

I could also say a big furry dog, with a chewy ball in his mouth, racing through a lush green pasture. Totally different imagery, right?

In both cases, I'm talking about a dog. But when I get specific, I really start to paint a picture in your mind. And that drives desire.

3. Primal desires

I believe the most powerful motivators of desire connect back to 3 primal desires: health, wealth, and love. These are universal touchpoints. We are all seeking them out. Depending on your target market, they can mean different things and have different levels of impact.

Health is a natural human concern. It could mean putting on muscle or losing weight. Some people may connect it with lack of illness. Others may associate it with running faster or jumping higher.

For many people, the concept of "wealth" has a strong tie to money. But for others it connects more to an abundance of time and freedom. I like to think of wealth as having a lot of the thing you want, whatever that thing is.

And love is at the center of human connection. Family, friendships, romance, communities. Getting along with your neighbors. Or being the popular kid in your high school.

Depending on the product or service you're selling, you can likely tie back to one of the 3 primal desires.

––––––

Taking another look at our AIDA example, let's sprinkle on some desire:

Attention: I just bought a private jet for $32

Interest: And you can get one right now for only $28

Desire: Imagine how much time you'll save with a private jet

Action:

Take a look at how I'm using the 3 methods for creating desire.

In this simple line, I'm using time travel. I'm suggesting that you imagine what your future could look like. Taking you to a moment in time, shortly after you've made your private jet purchase.

Then I'm digging deeper with one specific benefit. I'm not touching on comfort or status or prestige. I'm highlighting time. Perhaps I'm doing this because I know that's high on your list of priorities.

As for primal desires, this whole example touches on wealth. Since owning and using a private jet would clearly be a wealth indicator. And if you're still reading this piece of copy, I assume that your definition of wealth includes owning a private jet.

Mine certainly does!

Alright. If the reader is still with you, it's time to go in with our final move.

CHAPTER 39

Action

The hard work is all done. But the important work is just starting. Because the purpose of this copywriting is to get a response. We want action. That might mean getting a click, or making a sale, or locking in a new subscriber. Whatever it is, we need to make it happen.

The "action" is sometimes referred to as a "Call to Action" or CTA. (I'll use that acronym going forward).

Never assume your reader will know what to do. Even if you've mentioned it earlier in your writing. They may have forgotten. And although your action might be simple, it is critical. Without it, we have accomplished nothing. A word salad dumped onto a page that no one is going to eat. There are 3 things to keep in mind when writing your action statement:

1. Clear, not cute

The worst thing you can do now is try to get cute. Your action words don't need to be funny or cheeky or clever. They need to be clear. A 6-year-old should be able to read it and understand exactly what you're telling them to do. Don't be ambiguous. And don't make the reader wonder what they're supposed to do next. If they're confused, they're gone.

2. Reinforce the why

While I typically lean towards staying very short, it could make sense to reinforce the "why" in your CTA.

For example, if you're writing about why the reader should invest for their retirement, your CTA might be: "Call now to learn more."

Or you can reinforce the "why" by saying:

"Call now to learn how you can start investing for retirement today."

It's a subtle difference. But just saying those 8 words can nudge your reader over the edge. Those 8 words could be worth a lot of money.

3. Include the physical action

If you want to take it one step further, tell the reader exactly what physical action they should take in order to complete the CTA. This can sometimes sound patronizing when you're writing or saying it. But it doesn't come off that way to the reader.

I listen to podcasts quite a bit. And a typical CTA might sound like this:

"If you like this podcast, make sure to subscribe so you can get notified when we release a new episode."

That's a good CTA. It's clear and it reinforces the "why". But if you want to take it one step further, tell the reader what physical action they should take. I've heard this version and it works well:

"If you like this podcast, make sure to subscribe to get notified when we drop a new episode. Just take out your phone, tap the purple Podcast icon, find this show, and hit the Subscribe button."

You see how a description of the physical action makes it even more clear? We're saying something so obvious. After all, who doesn't know how to subscribe to a podcast?

You'd be surprised! Not everyone is as tech savvy as you might think.

Also, even someone who is tech savvy might procrastinate. A voice in their head says "good idea, I'll subscribe later". And then they never do. Opportunity gone.

By uttering the exact steps, you're giving them the nudge to actually do it.

Don't wait. Don't procrastinate. Don't hesitate. Take action right now.

_____

Let's complete the AIDA example with the Action step.

Attention: I just bought a private jet for $32

Interest: And you can get one right now for only $28

Desire: Imagine how much time you'll save with a private jet

Action: Take out your phone and text me so I can tell you how to get it. 212-555-9200.

I've packed in all the extras so you can see how they work. I start with the physical action: _take out your phone and text me._

Couldn't I just say "text me"? Sure I could. But maybe the reader is doing something else. They're distracted. Their little voice is saying "I'll do it later". Forget that. Do it now!

Next I reinforce the "why": _so I can tell you how to get it._

Don't they already know that's the reason for getting in touch? After all, I said that during Attention, Interest, and Desire.

Yes, but let's hit it again anyway. Don't let it fade into the background. The reason they're getting in touch is to get a private jet. Remind them.

Lastly, I drop my phone number. And then I'm done. No more information. I've put it all on the table. I snagged your attention, drummed up interest, stoked your desire, and gave you a clear action to take.

That's a crystal clear AIDA message. And it's the fundamental formula for all great copywriting.

Section 4: Recap

- Decide on the purpose, method, and form of your content
- Distribute your content through organic and paid channels
- Adjust your message based on where consumers are in the funnel:
  - ToFU
  - MoFU
  - BoFU
- Study my 7 ground rules of copywriting:
  - Grade 3 language
  - Tailor your lingo to the reader
  - Economy of words
  - Paint a picture
  - Start with action
  - Emotion first, logic second
  - Polarization is good
- Use the AIDA formula to write like a pro
  - Attention
  - Interest
  - Desire
  - Action

Bonus material:

To help you further, I made an AIDA cheat sheet. It's got the AIDA formula and an example so you can refresh your memory. There's also spots to practice by yourself.

Grab the worksheet now at JonDavids.com/MarketingSuperpowers.

Or snap the QR code below:

One more thing!

I hope you're getting a ton of value out of this book already. If you are, and you want to go deeper, you should take a look at my full training system, *Marketing Superpowers Pro*.

The system is designed for business builders and marketing professionals. It covers all the material in this book, and more. For example, I have a full session on copywriting that covers AIDA, plus 3 other frameworks that I use all the time.

You can learn more and enroll at **MarketingSuperpowersPro.com**

Congratulations on finishing Part 1 of Marketing Superpowers!

My goal is to help as many people as possible achieve their own marketing superpowers. And I need your help to do it.

If you're getting value out of this book, I'd love it if you could head over to Amazon and leave a review.

It doesn't have to be anything fancy. Just share something you've learned so far. When other people see your review, they might pick up a copy too.

Go to JonDavids.com/BookReview or snap the QR code below to leave a review now.

Thanks again. Now let's continue to Part 2.

MARKETING SUPERPOWERS

Part 2

SECTION 5

Your Unifying Belief

CHAPTER 40

My big break

I remember when I hit on my unifying belief. The exact moment I found the essence of my movement. It was a total breakthrough.

I made a piece of content about a company called Alo Yoga. It started like this:

Selena Gomez wears it. So does Kylie Jenner. And Gigi Hadid.

But this brand keeps that quiet. For good reason.

You won't find any of those ladies on its Instagram feed.

The brand I'm talking about is Alo, the yoga wear retailer that has exploded in popularity in spite of massive competition.

And they've done it in some not-so-obvious ways. Let me tell you about them.

I go on to talk about how Alo built a huge business on the power of their customer community. And I talk about how it's so important to lean on your customers to grow your brand. There's no other way to do it today.

And then I talk about how my agency Influicity, helps brands across the world, use the power of community to build their brand. It's my unifying belief, perfectly executed.

This piece of content performed very well, with over 356,000 people reading it.

You can read it on page 159. Or go to JonDavids.com/alo

Kylie Jenner wears it. So does Selena Gomez. And Gigi Hadid.

But this brand keeps that quiet. For good reason.

You won't find any of those ladies on its Instagram feed.

The brand I'm talking about is Alo, the yoga wear retailer that has exploded in popularity in spite of massive competition.

And they've done it in some not-so-obvious ways. Let me tell you about them.

1/ How it started

To understand Alo, lets rewind to 2007.

The company is co-founded by Danny Harris and Marco deGeorge. The two epitomize the brand ethos - practicing yoga daily, eating organic, and loving the outdoors.

They call their company Alo - an acronym for air, land, ocean.

And they're about to build a cult following.

2/ Building a Community

Alo embraces its tribe from day 1. They build a group of 4,000 yoga pros, who they partner with to create the content you see across social.

Their IG feed oozes SoCal yoga vibes. Sun soaked beaches, poolside palm trees, and plenty of in-studio shots.

Coupled with the perfect poses. Handstand scorpion, Lotus Legs, and Bhairavasana. All the good ones.

But zero famous faces -- and that's on purpose.

3/ Counter-Intuitive Influencer Strategy

The most fascinating part of Alo's strategy is how much restraint they have when it comes to influencers.

And as an influencer marketing OG, I find it kinda ridiculous. But I get it.

Here's the deal.

Celebrities like Selena, Gigi and Kylie are regularly spotted in Alo gear. So wouldn't it make sense to post some of those pics on the Insta feed?

Nope. Alo wants to focus on one thing - authentic yoga. That's all you're going to see here.

Deviating into celebrity culture puts them on a collision course with mass retail. That's not where they want to be.

4/ Stiff Competition

Lets state the obvious - LuluLemon should have crushed Alo long ago.

Or at least bought them. But it never did.

Alo found a niche and stuck with it. They've never tried to go full mainstream. It's for yogis, by yogis.

It helps that the business is still owned and funded by its founders. No shareholders and no board gives you the luxury to grow at your own pace.

5/ My Take

Alo is a brand that exemplifies community. And community is your most powerful weapon today.

We spent the last century glorifying the power of "brand". And for good reason. It's your most valuable intangible asset.

But it's not limited to your brand anymore. It's about your community. What people say about you when you're not looking. That's what matters.

Social is the new storefront. How you appear on Instagram and TikTok is exactly how you appear. Period.

Triple down on your community. That's what Alo did. And they've done pretty well with it.

10mo · Public post

❤️😮👍 1.4K · 103 comments · 56 reposts

Reactions

👍 Like   💬 Comment   🔁 Repost   ➦ Send

📊 356,502 impressions   View analytics

I had been building my brand and audience for a while. But this was the first time I really nailed the unifying belief. Finally, I was using my content to drive a specific, relevant message about my business.

If people liked the Alo story and they wanted to copy the Alo formula, I was telling them exactly how to do it.

Work with Influicity.

The response was swift and immediate. We had a dozen qualified prospects reach out to Influicity in the days following this post and 3 of them converted into clients.

I was creating a movement without even realizing it. This whole time, I had been providing a unique view on business building. I was reinforcing their faith in my perspective with frequent, high quality content. And now, people wanted to take action. Specifically, they wanted my team to work on their marketing.

CHAPTER 41

Building a unifying belief

The unifying belief is a big deal. It guides your movement and fuels your marketing superpower.

When I first developed the Movement Formula, I thought about the unifying belief almost like a mission statement, which Peter Drucker talked about back in the 1970's. While that's a good starting point, I actually don't think it's totally right. Drucker explained the mission statement as a way to "define the purpose and mission of the business as a strategic imperative."

I interpret that to mean the mission statement is for the *company*. Whereas my unifying belief is for the *customers*.

The customer doesn't care about *your* "why". They don't care about *your* anything. They don't even care that you exist. They care about themselves. Their wants. Their needs. Their dreams. Their desires.

It's about them.

And because of this, the unifying belief needs to check a few boxes. These are my 5 Belief Builders:

1. It must serve the customer

2. It must be within reach

3. It must be simple

4. It must be differentiated

5. It must be sustainable

Let's explore each of these right now.

CHAPTER 42

It must serve the customer

People are interested in solving their own problems. First and foremost. No exceptions, no substitutions. I want to make this clear off the top, because if you're under any other impression, you're probably going to conjure up some wishy-washy unified belief that sounds nice but accomplishes nothing.

You could cook up a grandiose statement about 'saving the world' or 'democratizing access' or whatever. But I suggest you leave these lofty thoughts at the door. Let's get real.

We'll start off with the thing you're selling. Identify your product or service.

Next, figure out what makes it unique. How does it stand out? This could be the product itself. Or it could be something outside that. Maybe it's the way you make it. Or how it works better. Or how it lasts longer. Or how it's easier than the other guys.

There are lots of ways to lose weight, but every method has its own unique path to get there.

- The Keto Diet pushes low-carbohydrate and high-fat to induce a state of ketosis, where the body primarily burns fat for energy. *And you'll lose weight.*

- The Mediterranean Diet emphasizes whole grains, fruits, vegetables, lean protein, and healthy fats. *And you'll lose weight.*

- The Paleo Diet focuses on foods that our ancestors might have eaten while avoiding processed foods, grains, and dairy. *And you'll lose weight.*

Do you see the pattern here? Each of these methods offers a different path – or unifying belief – that gets you to the same desirable outcome: *And you'll lose weight.*

The unifying belief must enhance something the customer wants (the good thing) or reduce something the customer hates (the bad thing). It should be visceral. The sharper, the better.

You shouldn't need to convince them that they want that thing. If that's what is required, you've chosen the wrong unifying belief or you've chosen the wrong customer. Some people think that if the movement is good enough, people who aren't otherwise interested will be convinced to jump on board.

Wrong.

It just doesn't happen like that. Even the greatest movement, with the strongest unifying belief, is not going to change someone's mind. That's not what it's designed to do. It's designed to get people who are interested in that outcome, to join your movement.

Your job is to meet them where they are today, and then move them.

I also want to emphasize that we're going after the selfish nature inside of everyone. We're not trying to appeal to what they *should* want. Or what we *wished* they wanted. It's what they actually want.

The thing they think about when no one else is looking or judging. What they want deep down. This is what drives them.

Once you have a unifying belief that serves the customer, you need to make sure they can actually achieve it.

CHAPTER 43

It must be within reach

Once we've identified a unifying belief that hits a nerve, we need to make sure it's attainable. People need to feel like they can actually achieve it. Not that they need to totally reinvent themselves or overhaul their life to get there.

It needs to feel like they can have it in a reasonable amount of time, with a reasonable amount of effort, for a reasonable cost.

We live in a button/swipe society. Your customer is literally a button or a swipe away from anything they want. A song, a date, a show, a sandwich, a ride. Anything. They're not looking to add something hard or inconvenient to their life.

So the ideal approach is to make your unifying belief effortless and immediate. Give people exactly what they want with zero work, right now.

But let's be honest, most things in life don't work like that. And I'll assume you can't realistically make that promise with your unifying belief.

What happens if the thing you're selling is expensive? Or time consuming? Or if it takes hard work? Or requires travel? Or sacrifice? I call these "downsides". And downsides are okay as long as there are relative upsides. A cost/benefit tradeoff.

Sticking with the weight loss example, no one thinks they're going to shed 10 pounds in 1 hour. That would be crazy. But they also don't want to wait a year to lose 1 pound. That would be unreasonable. The outcome needs to be within reach relative to the situation.

If there is a downside, you need to minimize it by providing a relative upside.

- If my product is *expensive*, I can push on quality and prestige

- If my service requires a lot of *time*, I can push on the long lasting results

- If my product requires *hard work*, I can push on the side benefits of that work

- If my service requires *training*, I can push on the pleasures of learning a new skill

I can also use this opportunity to review all my downsides and see how I can optimize my product offering. But that's something you should be doing all the time.

When you've settled on a unifying belief that serves the customer and that they can actually achieve, it's time to simplify.

CHAPTER 44

It must be simple

The greatest unifying beliefs are also the most simple. They're clear and succinct. If the unifying belief is complicated or confusing, you need to keep working on it. Remember, we're not developing a mission statement or a grand vision. These are tangible steps to enhance a good thing or reduce a bad thing.

Let's say I'm running a law firm. I help people get money from insurance companies after they've been in a car accident. And I have a track record of winning cases quickly so clients can get paid sooner.

My unifying belief could be:

- "Get the insurance money you're owed without the wait."

- "Get cash in your pocket, in months, not years."

- "It's already your money and you deserve it now."

A wishy-washy unifying belief might sound something like this: "I work hard to ensure all my clients get the justice they deserve."

That might be true. It might even be a nice mantra to hang in your lobby. But it doesn't resonate with me personally. I don't care about all your clients. And I don't know what "justice" means. But I do care about myself. And I know what "money" means.

When you keep it simple, you make it real.

CHAPTER 45

It must be differentiated

In order for your unifying belief to stand out, it must be different. If people already associate a unifying belief with one player, they're unlikely to abandon them for more of the same. Why would I drink "imitation cola" when Coke and Pepsi are within arm's reach? I won't.

The avenues of differentiation will vary depending on your market.

- If you're selling a fitness product, your way might be faster, cheaper, or take less effort.

- If you operate a coffee chain, your drinks may have more variety, nutritional benefits, or convenience.

- If you sell solar panels, they might be higher quality, longer lasting, or have a better certification.

The differentiation should give people more of the "good things" they want and less of the "bad things" they'd like to avoid.

The differentiation could also simply be a better product. While "better" is certainly different, the unifying belief needs to cut deeper than this. You need to ask yourself why. Unpack the rationale behind your unifying belief.

It's one thing to say "I make a better electric vehicle than what's currently on the market." That might be true, but why? Who is it better for? How durable is the improvement you've made? Can you quantify the improvement? Do you have evidence of the improvement?

As a rule, "better" is a tough difference to lean on. Unless you're selling something that is actually 10x better, I would look for another angle.

Once you go through this exercise, you'll start to craft a more meaningful, unifying belief that connects more deeply with your customer.

CHAPTER 46

It must be sustainable

I want to put this unifying belief through a time machine. Fast forward one year. Is it still relevant? Are people still interested in the promise you've made? Obviously we don't have a crystal ball, but we do have common sense.

We need to ensure that this thing has legs. That it will continue to resonate in a year from now, three years from now, five years from now. That's not to say we can't twist and tweak our unifying belief to stay with the times. But we don't want to do that on a monthly basis.

If your unifying belief hits on solid frameworks or fundamental human desires, you can be confident that it's sustainable. But if your path to get there is built on a trend or a tactic that will soon be outdated, you may want to reconsider.

At Influicity, we talk about building brands through the power of community so you can drive more revenue. And that means something specific today. We're talking about communities across social media, podcasts, Facebook groups, content creators, gaming platforms, chat platforms, and beyond. There are lots of ways to do marketing. We just tapped into the reality that society is more open today than ever. Your brand needs to be strong enough to survive in the wild. After all, you can't control what people say or how loud they say it. But if you build a strong community, you'll have a strong brand.

As things change with technology, trends, platforms, and behaviors, I'm sure that we'll need to update our unifying belief. But one thing is for sure – your brand will still need to survive in the wild. So our unifying belief will resonate. And when we do update it, we'll do it in small pivots rather than sudden jolts.

Make sure your unifying belief serves the customer, is achievable, is simple, and sustainable.

CHAPTER 47

Let's create a unifying belief together

We're going to run through an example of how I would develop a unifying belief. We'll start with an overview of a fictional company and then I'll lay out 5 ideas.

Next we'll explore each one together. And finally I'll give you my pick.

Here we go.

Overview:

I'm opening an ice cream shop. My focus will be on wacky flavors that are catchy, colorful, and camera-ready. We'll design the ice cream shop with the social media feed in mind. The walls will have graffiti and mirrors. Witty one-liners will sprawl across the ceilings. And we'll have an open kitchen where customers can watch the ice cream being made while they're in line.

For my unifying belief, I have a few options. At this point, I'm going to brainstorm different angles I can take based on the company overview. Here are some ideas that I can lean into:

1. Food is boring. Let's make it fun.

2. There's always room for dessert.

3. Be yourself, be authentic, be real.

4. Bring some excitement into your life.

5. Ice cream is bad for you. Let's make it healthy.

The first idea – *food is boring, let's make it fun* – is all about being creative with food. It might be interesting to people who are foodies or chefs.

Idea number two – *there's always room for dessert* – pushes on indulgence. It could have broader appeal to anyone with a sweet tooth.

At number three we have – *be yourself, be authentic, be real.* Now we're getting into personal empowerment and self-love. This message could appeal to people struggling with their self-confidence.

The fourth idea – *bring some excitement into your life* – speaks to the adventure-seeking crowd. It positions ice cream as an expression of adventure.

Idea number five – *ice cream is bad for you, let's make it healthy* – is about nutrition and diet. This would appeal to those who love ice cream but are trying to avoid it.

——

As you can see, each one of these touches on a specific feeling or emotion: creativity, indulgence, empowerment, adventure, and health. And as a result, they each target a different type of customer. Of course, there's overlap, but the focus of the unifying belief would be different in each example.

As a next step, we can run through the checklist and make sure each idea measures up against the 5 Belief Builders. I would say all of them pass.

They all serve the customer since each idea offers a distinct benefit that the intended customer would appreciate.

They're all within reach meaning a customer who eats our ice cream likely believes they can achieve that benefit.

They are simple enough to understand in just 1 or 2 sentences.

On differentiation, I think creativity and indulgence are the weakest. There are probably lots of ice cream shops that lean into those themes. Empowerment, adventure, and health are more differentiated.

And they're all sustainable since we could hit this messaging for a very long time. Even if the 'action' changes, the message would still resonate.

———————

At this point, it's time to pick one unifying belief. A lot of pressure, I know. But the good news is there's no wrong answer. It just depends on what sort of community you want to rally around your brand and ultimately who you want your customer to be.

Before you read on, I want you to pause and pick your own. I'll re-list them for quick reference:

1. Food is boring. Let's make it fun.

2. There's always room for dessert.

3. Be yourself, be authentic, be real.

4. Bring some excitement into your life.

5. Ice cream is bad for you. Let's make it healthy.

Here's a quick tip – jump back and read the overview again so you remember what kind of company we are building. Then write down your thoughts on each idea as a potential unifying belief.

Once you have your pick, read on to see how I approach it.

JD's approach to picking the unifying belief

My least favorite is number 5 – *ice cream is bad for you, let's make it healthy*. Given that my ice cream shop is all about wacky flavors and visual appeal, going with health as my unifying belief seems irrelevant.

Next I'm putting 2 more on the chopping block: *food is boring, let's make it fun* and *never skip dessert*. While either one could work as my unifying belief, they're not differentiated enough from other ice cream shops.

My runner up is clear – *bring some excitement into your life*. This one seems more differentiated since it targets adventure-seekers. And it fits nicely with the overview of the business.

But the unifying belief I'm going with is number 3: *be yourself, be authentic, be real*. The ice cream flavors are wacky and different. The vibe encourages people to express themselves and share visuals on social media. So a unifying belief of personal empowerment, self love, and overall positivity slides in nicely.

If you had a totally different perspective, that's cool. This is just an exercise with a fictional brand. A real brand that you're deeply connected with is a whole different game. Now you have a sense of how I approach it. And you can put your own spin on it.

Section 5: Recap

- Your unifying belief must:
    - be serving the customer
    - be within reach
    - be simple
    - be differentiated
    - be sustainable
- The unifying belief is not a mission statement. Focus on the customer's desires and needs, not those of the company.
- Handle the downsides by providing relative upsides.
- Generate multiple ideas and pick the one that makes the most sense. Don't rush it – this is important.

Bonus material:

I put together a checklist that you can use while developing your unifying belief. I find these checklists really helpful so I don't miss anything. I hope it helps you too!

Grab it now at JonDavids.com/MarketingSuperpowers.

Or snap the QR code below:

SECTION 6

Fuelling Faith

CHAPTER 48

You gotta have faith

After working on our unifying belief, we'll turn our attention to faith. This is the multiplier. It amplifies everything you do in step one and makes it monumentally more impactful.

So how do you fuel faith? The answer is *you* don't. Everyone else does it for you. Or at least, that's how you need to position it. In reality you are going to make it happen. Because you need to drive the process forward. But you can only create faith if others believe in the movement. If they're satisfied with the unifying belief (the promise) and the action (the product), we need to get them to say it.

There are two ways for strangers to truly develop faith:

1. When they hear about it from others

2. When they see undeniable proof with their own eyes

Other People

Faith is contagious. One person believes and they tell someone else. That person tells two more people. And the word continues to spread.

You know how restaurants become popular? By being so popular that you can't get a reservation. It's funny but it's true. Fans attract fans. Crowds attract crowds.

If we're on the fence about something, and then we see 100 other people who are really into that thing, we're going to feel a lot better about it. What if 1,000 people are into it? Or 10,000? It becomes almost impossible for us to resist.

- You're more likely to buy a specific toothpaste when "3,500 dentists recommend it".

- You're more likely to send your kid to a particular dance school, when every parent in the neighborhood sends their kid too.

- You're more likely to buy a specific car when the top car review site gives it 5 stars.

- You're more likely to see a movie when the movie reviews are all amazing.

Each of these 4 examples is actually a different kind of "other people". I call these the 4 Faith Groups. They are:

1. Real People

2. Authorities

3. Industry Groups

4. Media

We'll look at each one now and then cover how each one fits into our Faith playbook.

CHAPTER 49

Your 4 "Faith" Groups

1. Real People

Real people are the ones who look and sound like your target customer. The more similar, the better. They should represent the person you're trying to sell to. They should have similar challenges and issues. And they'll be in search of similar solutions.

That doesn't mean they should all be the same, of course. Because your customers are going to be diverse. So your "real people" should come from across the board and represent all the types of customers you have.

2. Authorities

The people that your "real people" look up to would be considered authorities. In the medical world, these might be doctors. In the technology world, these might be engineers. In the sports world, these might be professional athletes.

And it goes beyond that. You can think of social media influencers, podcasters, authors, academics, bloggers, and others. Anyone who is known to have an opinion in a category. Especially if they have a big audience.

3. Industry Groups

Most industries have groups that educate, review, certify, and/or award the companies in that industry. Some are very specific to that industry. And some are more broad.

While the public wouldn't necessarily know about your industry group, a review or award from that group can certainly create faith. If I tell you that my digital advertising agency was named the fastest growing digital agency by some group or association, it will amplify your faith.

Even if you've never heard of that group or association, it makes no difference. The acclaim means something.

I would also put accreditations in this category. If a group or institution gives you a certification of some sort, that helps. It's a badge you can slap on your website and it makes you look like the real deal.

4. Media

The media landscape has been changing rapidly for the last decade. And they're attracting a lot less eyeballs today than they did 20 years ago. But getting a call-out from traditional media still matters.

When you're featured in a newspaper or on the 6 o' clock news, is your target customer going to see it? Are they reading or watching at that moment? I have no idea. And it doesn't matter.

You get to clip that feature and post it everywhere. That matters. And that's why being featured by the media matters. It's not about distribution. It's about validation.

———

That's the "who". Next we'll talk about the "how".

How do you use these 4 faith groups to create faith? It's going to vary across the board. Your approach towards real people, authorities, industry groups, and media will each be different. You also don't need to engage all of them, all the time. There's a fit and a place for each.

In the next 10 chapters, I'll give you ten playbooks that you can use to build faith in different ways using a combination of all 4 faith groups.

Then you can pick and choose what makes sense for your brand and go all in. Let's do it.

CHAPTER 50

Review Sites

Who: real people

There are broad review websites like Yelp, Trust Pilot, and Google Reviews. And there are industry specific websites like Homestars (home repair), TripAdvisor (travel), G2 Crowd (software), RateMDs (doctors), and so on. Depending what industry you're in, you can decide where the bulk of your potential customers are seeing reviews.

To get a review, you just need to ask. I like to ask customers for a review at a moment when I know they are most likely to do it. In a short term engagement, this can be at the end of the job. In a long term engagement, it can be at the first check-in. Perhaps one month or one quarter after starting your work together.

To get a review, send an email to your customer and ask how things are going. Assuming things are going well, send another email saying this:

I'm so glad to hear things are going well so far. If you have a moment, I'd love it if you could leave a review on [review site].

I know a lot of others are struggling with similar challenges and would benefit from just a few words sharing your experience. It doesn't need to be perfect — anything you're comfortable sharing.

Here's a link: [insert link to review site]

Thank you!

If you want to kick it up a notch, send the same email but include a $5 gift card. The act of sending a small gift will generate natural feelings of reciprocity and make it even more likely that they'll take action. And if not, it's not a big deal. Just a $5 gift to a current customer.

Some people feel like this is a bribe. I assure you, it's not. If this customer genuinely wasn't happy with your service they won't leave a positive review. So you're not forcing them into doing something disingenuous. You're simply nudging them along.

★★★★★   Jul 10, 2023

A lovely experience!

I visited SW3 with my daughters and we all thoroughly enjoyed the experience. We were given clear information about what to expect and how to prepare for the day, from the moment we were considering buying the experience (at the Ideal Home Show) through to booking our date and time.
In addition, our host, Leah, called me on the morning of our experience, to check what my daughter with food allergies (dairy and gluten) could and couldn't eat, as we were also having an afternoon tea included. When it came to that time in the day, my daughter had as lovely an afternoon tea as my other daughter and I enjoyed.
Everyone involved in our day - host, hair, makeup, photographers - was really friendly, welcoming and asked us what we wanted throughout. We never felt rushed at any point. We came away with some beautiful photos and memories of a unique day together.

Date of experience: July 05, 2023

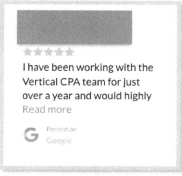

★★★★★

I have been working with the Vertical CPA team for just over a year and would highly
Read more

G Posted on
Google

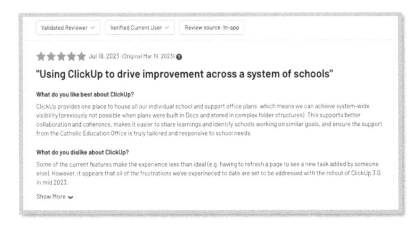

★★★★★ Jul 18, 2023 (Original Mar 19, 2023) ❓

"Using ClickUp to drive improvement across a system of schools"

What do you like best about ClickUp?

ClickUp provides one place to house all our individual school and support office plans, which means we can achieve system-wide visibility (previously not possible when plans were built in Docs and stored in complex folder structures). This supports better collaboration and coherence, makes it easier to share learnings and identify schools working on similar goals, and ensure the support from the Catholic Education Office is truly tailored and responsive to school needs.

What do you dislike about ClickUp?

Some of the current features make the experience less than ideal (e.g. having to refresh a page to see a new task added by someone else). However, it appears that all of the frustrations we've experineced to date are set to be addressed with the rollout of ClickUp 3.0 in mid 2023.

Show More ⌄

★★★★★   Jun 19, 2023

Lovely mother daughter day @ SW3

Lovely mother daughter day @ SW3. The whole team were so lovely & attentive, from the host, manicurist, makeup artist & photographer and Sam who made the process of picking photos a joy. Have been to another makeup/hair & photo session and hated the whole experience, makeup awful, photos awful and way too my pressure to sell package. Thank you SW3 for changing my experience. My 15 year old daughter was made to feel like a model and I'm awful in front of the camera but Mateo just made me feel comfortable and we walked away with some Beautiful memories. My makeup was done beautifully and not caked on. Had a lovely afternoon tea and my gluten free daughter was catered for. Thank you all for a fab day!

Date of experience: June 17, 2023

Powder/Laundry Room Remodel   **10/10**

Kitchen Planning & Renovation review in Toronto   4 months ago

Sterling and his crew were amazing to work with. They did a great job and everyone was happy and a pleasure to be around. Most importantly, when a few things went sideways, as they do when renovating, Sterling was determined to make everything as perfect as possible. I will definitely call Arkhitekton for my next project!

Job Price ⌄

Was this review helpful?   Yes   No

f 🐦

✎ **Company Response**

Thank you Stuart. Look forward to working with you again!

Reviews from real people are critical for creating faith

CHAPTER 51

Interview testimonials

Who: real people, authorities

In an interview testimonial, you can ask a series of questions that are all designed to elicit a meaningful response. This leads to some of the most authentic, genuine testimonials you can possibly get.

Let's say you own a baking school called *Sweet Success Baking School.* Here are 5 questions you could ask a customer in an interview to get a strong testimonial:

1. What was the problem you had before joining Sweet Success Baking School?

2. Why did you choose Sweet Success over any other school?

3. As a result of implementing our lessons, what was the outcome and how has it made your life different?

4. Where do you think you'd be right now if you didn't join Sweet Success?

5. If there's anyone watching this who is on the fence about joining Sweet Success, what would you tell them?

You see how those questions go beneath the surface? The answers would be far more insightful to a potential customer than a generic review, like "I love your company!"

We're getting specific. We're making it useful. That's going to build a lot of faith.

You can also do an interview testimonial with an authority, like an influencer or an industry specialist. These people don't need to be your customers. Instead, you can just ask what they think about your product in general.

For example, you can ask questions like "Why do you think our approach makes more sense for people?" Or "Why do most people fail when they try this?"

Coming from an authority, the answers to these questions will resonate with your potential customers.

You can record the interview testimonial as a video and then release it on your website or YouTube. Then you can chop it up into clips and release individual questions and answers. You can also transcribe it and put the written version on your website. And you can snap a screenshot of the customer with a powerful quote on top of the photo. Now you have loads of content to share in loads of places.

The interview testimonial provides a ton of flexibility, builds authenticity, and brings real insight for potential customers.

CHAPTER 52

Check-in testimonials

Who: real people

Moving to the less traditional, the "check-in testimonial" can yield some juicy results. This is where you email a customer during a normal check-in or after you've completed a task, and simply ask how things are going.

- Were you happy with our work around [task]?

- Did we deliver [task] as you were expecting?

- Was there anything else you needed regarding [task]?

If you've done the task to their satisfaction, they'll likely respond with something like:

- You did a great job!

- Thanks, you guys did exactly what we wanted!

- I always appreciate your great work!

Now you just screenshot that message and you've got yourself a check-in testimonial.

At Influicity, we grab screenshots like this all the time and put them in a shared team folder. That way, when we need testimonials for a presentation, brochure, or webpage, we have lots.

Here are some samples I pulled. Both of these clients work with Influicity to produce their company podcasts.

To: Jon Davids,

Thanks Jon!

Dillon and Mackenzie have been very helpful to make this first episode happen.

Thanks so much Jon. Your team did a stellar job in turning things around and taking feedback and actioning it quickly.

🙂

nb

Here are some examples we pulled from our Slack channels. We use Slack to talk to our clients. So when they say something nice, again, we screenshot it!

You can do this with emails, message boards, group chats, and any other communication platform you use with your clients.

CHAPTER 53

Testimonials from Authorities

Who: authorities

An authority is anyone that your customer looks to for guidance. This could be social media influencers, trade groups, industry professionals, or rating agencies. I also include industry awards and accolades in this category.

Engaging these types of authorities can be done for free or for a fee.

At Influicity, we work with brands all over the world, building influencer programs to drive their brand message. This is mostly pay-to play. These social media influencers definitely love the brand, but they are paid to share the message with their followers.

Trade groups and industry professionals can be engaged with no exchange of money. For example, if you sell a teeth-whitening product, you can invite 100 dentists to a private party, wine and dine them, demonstrate the product, and hopefully get a bunch of them to say how great it is on camera. Then you can make the statement "100 dentists recommend my teeth-whitening product".

I know this sounds overly simple, but that is actually how a lot of those sorts of claims are made.

Rating agencies are different for each industry and oftentimes they get paid to rate your product or service. If your industry has a specific rating agency, it could be worthwhile to engage them. But it really depends on how much weight your potential customers put into that rating.

Similarly, industry awards and accolades are a great way to establish credibility. If you win an award, get a certification, make it onto a list, or anything like that, tell the world. Throw it on your website, put it in your email signature, and shout it from the rooftops. I'm pretty sure 80% of those awards are meaningless, but don't let that get in the way.

Let the world know.

CHAPTER 54

User Generated Content

Who: real people

Let's break down each word in "user generated content".

First we have "user". This could refer to any person from a customer to a prospective customer to some random dude on the internet.

Next is the word "generated". This means the user is the one making something.

And finally, the thing they're making is "content". That could be a video, photo, blog post, or some other type of content.

Put it together and we have user-generated content or UGC for short.

In the broadest sense, any content about your brand or product that is made by someone who doesn't need to be making that content, is UGC. Something like a review or testimonial is a type of UGC. And there are so many more.

When someone shares a photo on Instagram talking about a great hotel they're staying at, that's UGC for the hotel. When they leave a review for the hotel on a travel site. That's UGC. When they do a video tour of the hotel on YouTube, that's UGC.

UGC is powerful because it's real. It's authentic. It's content that looks like it was made by a real person, about a real thing, purely because they like that thing. And it looks that way because it's true!

The real power in UGC is not just in the content, but in the volume. Lots of UGC gives the perception that a lot of people are really enjoying this product or service. So much that they're telling everyone about it. This fuels social proof, which is incredibly powerful in creating faith. When others are researching this hotel, they'll come across the UGC all over the place. And it adds major credibility.

After all, this isn't the company talking about how great they are. Ordinary people are hyping it up.

To get UGC, make it easy for people to make it.

If you have a physical space, you can set aside an area that is camera-ready. Anyone can take a second to snap photos and videos. You can have your name and logo in the background. And then a sign that tells people how to tag you in their post. For example, if they're sharing the photo on Instagram or TikTok, they can input your username when they upload your content. Or they can include your hashtag.

If you are a virtual company with no physical space, you can encourage people to feature your product via your website, social media, or email.

I encourage you to build this into your communication process. One of our clients is a mid-size retailer. They have hundreds of customers passing through their physical and online store daily. One time, I walked in and made a purchase. The lady behind the counter handed me the receipt and I couldn't believe what I saw. More accurately, I couldn't believe what I didn't see. The receipt didn't tell me how or where I should share my love for this brand on social media.

I told the head of marketing right away. The next day, they added one line to the bottom of their receipt:

What do you think of our product? Tell us on Instagram! Tag us @_____.

Within days they were seeing dozens of happy customers tagging them on the platform. One line of text leads to tons of UGC.

When people do create UGC, show your gratitude. You can do this by sending a thank you message on the same platform and by reposting their content to your channel. Not only is this a great way to show your thanks, but it also reinforces faith to everyone else.

It's a virtuous cycle. Don't let it stop.

CHAPTER 55

Influencer Marketing

Who: authorities

We've been doing influencer marketing for a decade at Influicity. So I could write a whole book on how influencers amplify faith. I probably will one day. But the short version goes like this.

Influencers have a reputation among their followers for knowing or doing something specific. And there are influencers in pretty much every category. Fishing, medicine, food, travel, climate, farming, design. You name it, there's a content creator with an audience.

You can work with these people on a paid engagement or by sending them products and hoping they will talk about it. At Influicity, we recommend the first one because it's much easier to manage, measure, and monitor. Sending a free product is like marketing with a hope and a prayer. It works sometimes, but it doesn't scale.

We also recommend that influencer marketing should be done on a continual basis. It's not a start/stop kind of thing. At least not if you want to achieve serious momentum.

If you're willing to pay influencers, take a close look at their audience and engagement on a per post basis. For example, if they post content on Instagram, how many likes, comments, and shares are they getting per post? As a general rule, 2% is a very good engagement rate. So if an influencer has 100,000 followers, they should get 2,000 likes, comments, and shares combined on an average post.

But this does vary across the board. The engagement rate can go up or down depending on category, frequency of posting, length of time on that platform, and many other factors. This will be different for every business and I obviously can't cover every variable here.

So here's a universal rule that will help you evaluate things for yourself.

Don't look at just one influencer. Look at lots. There's power in numbers. When you have your heart set on one influencer, you have no context for what things should cost and how they should perform. When you have 10 influencers or 100 influencers, you have much better visibility. You're not just relying on the word of one person, you're looking at the data of many.

To connect with influencers, you can reach out by direct messaging them on their social platform or sending an email.

And if you have a bigger budget, I would strongly recommend working with an agency. It'll save you loads of time and money, while giving you more access and data to back up your decisions. There's a ton of expertise that goes into influencer marketing with bigger budgets.

If you are not planning to pay influencers, many of the tactics are the same. The only difference is you'll spend more time reaching out and getting rejected because there's less incentive for them to work with you. Offer them free products, discounts, or a share of the revenue if they refer customers. Anything that makes it worth their time.

And be prepared for high volume outreach. Influencer marketing can be a grind. But it moves the needle big time.

CHAPTER 56

Media mentions

Who: media

A media mention can vary from something tiny to something huge. It could be a reference to your product in a list. It could be you giving a comment on a news event. Or maybe it's a featured interview where you're on the cover of a national magazine.

These are all media mentions, of various significance.

Getting mentioned in the media is good for two reasons. First, you'll get seen by all the people who consume that particular media, whether it's a news site, a TV show, a podcast or some other outlet. But more importantly, it lets you pull the image, quote, or clip from that media mention and use it in your promotional material.

When you go to a company's website and you see logos for magazines and news channels who have talked about that company, it creates faith that a media outlet has praised them. Even in the age of media skepticism, where people love to bash the media for being untrustworthy, it still matters.

Getting the media to talk about you comes down to getting on their radar. And in many cases, it's about being in the right place at the right time. That doesn't mean it's about luck. Not at all. It's actually about persistence. Building a reputation as someone that reporters can call on for an opinion, an interview, a statement, or a comment when it makes sense.

Professionals who get you media attention are called "publicists". And the best publicists I know are great at two things:

1. Positioning you and your company as an expert in your category.

2. Getting in front of reporters when there's a news story that overlaps with your particular category.

If you have a budget for this, go ahead and hire a publicist. If not, here's how you can get media mentions on your own.

Start by creating a spreadsheet with 3 columns:

1. Media Outlet

2. Contact

3. Email

In the first column, list all the media outlets that matter in your space. Cast a wide net including magazines, newspapers, blogs, podcasts, radio shows, newscasts, TV shows, and more.

In the second column put the names of the reporters, journalists, writers, and producers who make decisions on who and what to feature. For written media like magazines and blogs, you can just look at the name of the writer who covers your "beat". A beat is reporter lingo for their area of specialization, like retail or consumer technology. Reporters spend time developing expertise and sources for their beat. So you want to get into their circle.

For non-written media like your local newscast or a radio show, the person on the air isn't always the one deciding who or what gets on the air. That would be the producer. To find out who the producer is, just listen to or watch the credits. On radio and podcasts, they'll usually call out their producer at some point. Listen for it and grab their name. On TV, you'll see the names at the end of the show. These are the people you need to know.

Finally, in column three you need to add email addresses. A lot of the time, these are easy to find since these people actually do want to be contacted. Check the websites or if there's a phone number, just call and say you're a publicist and you're updating your contact database. They'll be happy to give you a current email address.

Once you've done all this, the real work starts. Get into the habit of sending regular emails with research, announcements, awards, and pitches for stories they might want to cover.

You can get really creative with media outreach. I have a friend who owns a fireworks company. Every summer, when fireworks sales are picking up, he sends out a report to his media list outlining how many fireworks he's selling per week. When they're doing stories around Fourth of July celebrations, they'll often quote his company with the fireworks sales numbers.

Does one guy with a fireworks stand have any authority when it comes to national fireworks sales? Maybe not. But with that kind of media attention, people sure have faith in him.

The last point I want to emphasize on media mentions is just to make it easy for the media to work with you. They want to capture attention and they need to hit their deadlines.

The people and companies who get quoted in the media aren't necessarily the biggest or the best. They're the ones who make it easy to do a great story. After all, that's what the media is looking for. So make sure your business is relevant, interesting, and timely.

When the media is looking for a good story, you want to be on speed dial.

CHAPTER 57

Awards

Who: industry groups, media

If you want to rack up some prestige, dust off your trophy case and get ready to fill it up. There are so many groups today who dole out awards. Magazines, newspapers, websites, newsletters, industry organizations with confusing acronym names. There are even groups that are solely set up to give out awards.

Awards get a bad wrap because a lot of time, it's pay-to-play. They're a money grab where you need to pay money to be considered and therefore, it's not a true sampling of all the potential companies. Rather, just those companies who forked up the cash to be included.

I'm not saying this to knock awards, I'm just highlighting the criticism that a lot of people have towards them. So here's what I really think: It doesn't matter. Your potential customers will see an award badge or "best-of" on your website and they'll be impressed. Plain and simple. At the very least, they won't be unimpressed.

If the award is 100% merit-based, good on you. And if it's not, good on you for being savvy enough to apply for (and win) an award.

To search out awards in your industry, just do a web search. Type out your industry and the word "awards". I bet you'll find various awards, in various cities, given out by various organizations. You may need to go through a lengthy submission process or it might take just a few clicks.

And it could be well worth it.

CHAPTER 58

Certifications

Who: industry groups

Similar to awards, certifications come in all shapes and sizes. Some are extremely valuable, like a Harvard diploma. And some you can get by going to YouTube University and answering some multiple choice questions. Congratulations, you're certified.

The nice thing about certifications is you can learn something new. But more importantly, you can place the badge on your marketing material: your website, brochures, client presentations, social media channels, and so on. Tell the world that you passed this exam or achieved that accreditation. And now your company is qualified to do something special.

Depending on your industry, the certification might be administered by a trade group, college, or industry association. Just do a web search by typing your industry and the word "certification".

Learn something new and tell the world.

CHAPTER 59

Case studies

Who: real people

Nothing builds faith quite like a solid track record. If I'm paying someone to defend me in a lawsuit or do surgery to fix my knee ligament, I want to know they've done it before. And I'm not relying on the honor system. I want proof. Hard evidence. I want to know exactly what they've done and how well they did it.

The same is true in all businesses. That's why we have case studies.

A case study is an analysis of a specific client situation, focusing on the challenge faced, actions taken, and outcomes achieved. This can be as high-level or as in-depth as you need it to be, to get the point across.

If you're an interior designer, your case studies could be 90% visual, showing before-and-after photos with bits of text to help tell the story. You'll highlight colors, fixtures, and fabrics. You might add some timelines and talk about the inspiration behind your designs.

If you're an aerospace manufacturer, your case studies would be jam-packed with technical specifications, performance metrics, compliance protocols, and more. It would be dense with charts, graphs, and tables. Anything less wouldn't be sufficient.

Every company will approach case studies differently. But I've got two words that should be front and center in your mind: *Undeniable Proof.*

You want to get as close to undeniable proof as you possibly can.

When someone is reviewing your case study, it should make them feel like you are a total pro at this one thing. That trusting you is a no-brainer. Because not only have you done this, you've done it many times before. And if they choose to work with you, they'll be in very good hands.

To create your case studies, first decide on a format. It can be text, photo, video or a combination. It can be a single sheet or a multi-page report. And you can have different case studies in different formats.

At Influicity, we have case studies on our website that are done with text and photos. We have video case studies that tell a story in 1 minute. And we have detailed case studies that are written more like reports. Depending on the use-case, we can share the best one with our client.

Once you have a format, tell the story by answering these 3 questions:

1. What was the challenge?

2. What strategy/action did you implement?

3. What was the outcome?

The more effectively you can answer these 3 questions, the better your case study will be.

If you have permission, you can reveal the name of your client. Or you can choose to keep that confidential. So you might say "here's what we did for our client Toyota" or "here's what we did for our client, a global car maker". You pack a little more punch by name-dropping a reputable brand. But you also need to maintain the confidentiality of your client. So don't overshare.

Pump out case studies as often as you can. The more the better. Each one creates just a little more evidence that you're the real deal.

―――――

I want to leave you with one final thought on this section: *Faith is a multiplier.* Anything and everything you can do to drive up faith, multiplies the effect of the unifying belief. And this leads to way more action.

The impact of faith is not cumulative. When done properly, it's exponential.

―――――

Section 6: Recap

- Faith is built through the influence of four key groups: Real People, Authorities, Industry Groups, and Media.
- Real People are your customers and prospective customers. They should be diverse yet relatable.
- Authorities are people or groups that are well-known and respected in your industry, such as thought leaders and influencers.
- Industry Groups are organizations that educate, review, and award companies in a specific industry.
- Media includes magazines, newspapers, blogs, podcasts and publications that reach your target customers.
- I outlined 10 ways to engage with these various faith groups. They are:
  - Review Sites
  - Interview Testimonials
  - Check-in Testimonials
  - Testimonials from Authorities
  - User Generated Content
  - Influencer Marketing
  - Media Mentions
  - Awards
  - Certifications
  - Case Studies

Bonus material:

I created a checklist of the 4 Faith Groups and 10 Faith Drivers for easy reference. Use this checklist to mix and match the best combination as you build out faith for your movement.

It's actually the same checklist from Section 5. But if you didn't grab it then, get it now at JonDavids.com/MarketingSuperpowers.

Or snap the QR code below:

SECTION 7

Action

CHAPTER 60

Money Moves

It's time to go deeper into the money side of your movement. That's where the action comes in. If you've been effective at creating a unifying belief and multiplied it with faith, people will want to take action.

The purpose of *(1) the unifying belief* and *(2) faith that this is the best way to do it,* is ultimately to *(3) drive an action.* That action should be the thing you're selling.

Let me put that another way. You create the first thing and fuel the second thing, so you sell the third thing.

Here's an example:

I'm building a movement around the nutritional benefits of dark chocolate. It's rich in antioxidants, contributes to heart health, controls your appetite, improves your skin, and more. That's my unifying belief. I scream it from the rooftops.

Plus, I have case studies and testimonials from 100's of people who are die-hard, dark chocolate lovers. I have expert testimonials, research studies, and certifications from two public health institutes. These are my faith drivers.

So where's the action? I'm selling a line of dark chocolate. Duh. It's not just any dark chocolate. It's the perfect dark chocolate. It's award-winning dark chocolate. It's my dark chocolate. Certified, verified, and stamped with the seal of approval of the only person that matters.

Me.

Because I'm the main character of the movement.

And no. I don't actually sell dark chocolate. But if I did, it would be delicious.

You see how the action is the money? And the money is the action?

When you are the person or brand creating a unifying belief in the market, customers will always be inclined to buy from you. Sometimes, they'll be more than inclined. They will beat a path to your door. That all depends on how much faith they have.

That's why the Movement Formula is:

Unifying Belief x Faith = Action.

Faith is the multiplier. The more faith you achieve, the greater the unifying belief, and the more action people take.

That's why I'm a big believer in delivering tons of value in the form of content. Give away your content freely and abundantly. Get it in front of people who can benefit from it. Don't try to sell anything. They'll see right through that. Provide value and validation, while asking for nothing in return. Do this as best you can for as long as you can.

Build up the belief and multiply it with faith. When you do those two things, the action will follow. And that means money.

CHAPTER 61

Product Path: Turning a Movement into Money

I want to go deeper into exactly how your movement becomes a marketing strategy that can drive sales. It sounds simple, but a lot of businesses get scrambled at this point.

Here's why.

If you're selling a physical product, like tires, vitamins, or laptops, the path of movement to money seems clear-cut. I build a movement around the benefits of my product and then I sell my product. Not complicated.

But what if you're selling an information product? Say you're a lawyer or a nutritionist. The thing you're selling is your knowledge. How are you supposed to create lots of content with tons of value, and not give away the very thing you want people to pay for?

If I want you to pay me for investment advice, but I'm giving it away for free, why would you ever buy it?

And what if I'm selling a service like plumbing or auto repair? If I create content revealing how the work is done, wouldn't you just do it yourself?

These are common roadblocks that keep businesses from providing true value in the form of content.

I'll break down exactly how to do it the right way. I call this my *Product Path*.

There are 3 ways to look at making content depending on the nature of your business:

1. If you are **selling a physical product**, your content is about the product benefits, how to use the product, how to get more value out of the product, and so on. No holding back. *And then you sell the physical product itself.*

2. If you are **selling a service**, your content is about the service benefits, how to get the most value out of the service, and how to do it all yourself (if possible). *And then you sell the implementation.*

3. If you are **selling an information offering**, your content is about the benefits of that information, how to get the most value out of the information, and high level explanations of the information. *And then you sell the how.*

I call this my *Product Path* because it's literally the path a customer takes from your movement to your product.

Let's look at each one in more detail.

CHAPTER 62

Selling a physical or digital product

I start with this one because it's the most straightforward example. When you're selling a product, you don't need to worry that someone will go around you and hack together a solution. Not that they couldn't possibly do that, it's just unlikely.

Let's say I'm selling accounting software. We'll call it NumberSoft. You need to buy a license or subscription to NumberSoft in order to use it. Simple as that.

I'm not concerned that you're going to build your own accounting software. The more legitimate concern would be that you would not use accounting software at all. Or that you would choose a competitor's software. And this is the real mission my movement serves.

I want you to understand the benefit of using software over no software. And the benefit of using NumberSoft over some other software.

So I'll create a unifying belief with topics like:

- Why you need to know your numbers to win in business

- How to quickly create a cash flow projection

- How to read a profit & loss statement

- How to do your taxes in 5 easy steps

- What your accountant will never show you (but you need to see)

- 3 numbers that reveal everything (and where to find them)

Then I'll drive faith in that unifying belief with testimonials, reviews, case studies, awards, UGC, and so on.

The thing to remember is this: My product is a key ingredient to my unifying belief. It's the elixir. It's the one thing that makes magic happen.

My content is pushing my unified belief and providing real value. It's not a sales pitch. I'm just trying to help people. And if they want to take full advantage of the help I'm providing, they need to take action. The best way to take action is by purchasing NumberSoft.

Again, this is a clear-cut example because I'm selling a digital product. The same logic applies to physical products like food, furniture, and anything else you hold in your hand.

Let's take it one step further. Suppose I'm selling a service.

CHAPTER 63

Selling a service

With a service offering, business owners start to tighten their grip on doling out information. Their logic is, if I tell you what to do, you won't need my service. You'll just do it yourself.

This is bogus logic. Think about it for a moment. Do you really believe the one thing standing between your customer and your service is that they don't know what to do? Seriously?

Don't you think they could do a Google search? Or go to YouTube University? Or buy a book? Or ask a friend who has done it before?

Of course they could! There are a hundred ways that your potential customer could figure out what to do. But that's not the thing standing in the way of them doing it.

People buy services for so many reasons.

- Because they don't want to do it themselves.

- Because they want a first-class experience.

- Because they don't trust themselves to do it.

- Because they want guaranteed outcomes.

- Because they're too lazy to do it.

- Because they don't have time to do it.

- Because they want peace of mind.

- Because they're not qualified to do it.

These are just some of the reasons they are choosing to work with you. So don't be afraid to tell them exactly what you're going to do. Be generous with your information. The more generous the better, since they'll realize how robust your knowledge is. And they'll know they couldn't possibly do the thing at the same level as you.

At that point, you sell them the implementation. The delivery of the actual service. That's the thing they want from you.

Let's go back to my NumberSoft example. But instead of accounting software, suppose NumberSoft is a full-service accounting firm. We do your bookkeeping, payroll, tax planning, audits, and more.

I can use a lot of the same content from the previous example to create a unifying belief. And I can drive faith with the same testimonials and success stories.

But in this case, the action would be to work with the NumberSoft accounting firm. If we reinforce why it's so important (the unifying belief) and all the people who love our work (the faith), potential customers will naturally take action.

And that action will be working with NumberSoft.

Now that we've covered the product path for a product and a service, we'll look at the last one. An information offering.

CHAPTER 64

Selling information

Businesses who sell information are notoriously tight with that information. They're secretive. They're vague. They don't want to say much of anything because if they do, why would you pay them?

Again, this is limited thinking. And it holds them back from the movement they could be building if they shifted to an abundance mindset.

There are 3 ways to create high-value content if you're in the business of selling information.

The first is to cover the 3 W's: what, why, and who. Create content around what information you sell, why it's so important, and who needs to hear it.

Continuing with the example of NumberSoft, let's say I'm selling a course teaching businesses how to do their accounting internally. I could create content around the *what, why, and who:*

- Why your business must take control of its accounting

- What accounting firms never tell you about your numbers

- Who should be managing the books in your company

- Why so many firms are in-sourcing their accounting

- Who needs to know which numbers in any business

- Why not knowing your numbers is a dangerous mistake

This content is powerful in galvanizing and rallying people behind my unifying belief. It works very well. But it's surface level. I'm not actually giving you game-changing information. Where's the juice? Where's my mind-blowing content?

Let's kick it up a notch with my second method. What if we just give away the information? Take a chunk of our course, which we charge money for, and just give it away? That would be super valuable. So let's do it.

If you have a course with 10 lessons, take the first lesson and make it free. Just make sure it's really good. Give people something that they can use right now. With a measurable outcome. If lesson 1 is great, why wouldn't they buy lessons 2-10?

If you don't want to give away lesson 1, then just take a portion of lesson 1 and go in-depth on it. Dissect it, analyze it, cut it to the bone. Give your customer a world-class education on one tiny thing. Again, it needs to be remarkable.

If my NumberSoft course covers Corporate Accounting, maybe I'll give away Lesson 1: *The Fundamentals of Corporate Accounting*. If I don't want to give away all of Lesson 1, I can give away one slice of it: *Understanding Double-Entry Accounting*.

You can decide exactly what to offer. But this can't be fluff. It needs to be solid information.

And I've got one more method for you. Here's number 3.

If you're selling a Corporate Accounting course, you can create free content about the things people need to know *just before* they take a Corporate Accounting course.

Perhaps you could do a mini-course on Financial Literacy. Not only are you providing value, but you're actually attracting people who might not feel qualified to take your Corporate Accounting course yet.

You're giving them the basics they need to instill confidence, so they can move ahead.

———

As a recap, if you're selling an information offering, you can still give away information. Three types of information are:

1.   The 3 W's: what, why, who

2.   The first piece of valuable information

3.   Information needed *just before* the information you're selling

There's so much information to give, and so many ways to do it. Don't be afraid to over-deliver on value upfront. You'll create tons of goodwill and people will feel much more confident handing over their money when they see how good your free stuff is.

CHAPTER 65

Putting it all together

At this point, you have all the information you need to ignite your movement. Here's a quick recap:

- We reviewed the movement formula: Unifying Belief x Faith = Action

- We discussed how to craft each one of those ingredients

- We looked at the different types of content, tailored to a product, service, or information offering.

- And we wrapped all of this in communication tactics to get your message to the masses.

You could stop reading right now and start making your movement a reality. And I hope you do. Because it will turbocharge your business on many levels. But hang on – we're actually not done yet.

Because I don't just want you to have a powerful movement that drives revenue. I want you to make a ton of money. Obscene amounts. And to do that, you need to step up the action. Give your customers more value as their needs elevate.

And that's why we need to talk about the product ladder.

CHAPTER 66

The Product Ladder

Feb 24, 2017

9:52am.

I'm feeling confident. We're 90% to the finish line. We've given them everything they asked for. Now it's time to close.

Influicity just pitched a prospective client. It was intense. High stakes. This is a global real estate company. They own skyscrapers, shopping centers, and apartment buildings. And they want us to run their influencer marketing. Using content creators to promote their destinations.

We've been speaking with them for 5 months. And they'll be responding to us today. I'm refreshing my email every 23 seconds. Once this deal comes through – and I know it will come through – it will crank Influicity to a new level.

A huge client. A game changer. Best of all, we came in under budget. I know they'll choose us.

10:17am.

I refresh my inbox. There it is. The email I've been waiting for. I click it. And my eyes jump straight to the important part.

While we appreciate you taking the time to speak with us…

My heart sinks. This sentence can't possibly end well.

Blah, blah, blah. We're going with another partner.

Damn it. What did we do wrong? I keep reading.

While we know Influicity is a leader in influencer marketing, we wanted to go with an agency who also has expertise in paid advertising and social media management.

Wait, what? So they didn't pass on us because of what we offer. Or because of our track record. Or because of our price. They passed because we're not offering enough?! These guys have plenty of money to spend and we don't have enough to sell them.

They're not trying to save money. They're trying to spend more! And get more value in return.

And Influicity lost. I lost.

That day changed everything. And it opened my eyes to the power of the Product Ladder.

CHAPTER 67

What is the Product Ladder

Imagine a ladder that goes from the floor up to the ceiling. The first rung of the ladder is 2 feet off the ground. Low enough for anyone to step on.

The next rung is 2 feet above that. The third rung is 2 feet above that. And so on. The rungs go to the top of the ladder. So depending on how high you'd like to climb, there's a rung for you.

Want to put something onto a shelf 7 feet high? The first or second rung should get you to a comfortable spot. But maybe you need to change the light bulb on the ceiling? Then you'll need to head up to the top.

The point is, it's your choice. I'm giving you a ladder, you pick the rung.

Now imagine that ladder is your product offering. Each rung represents a version of your product and a price point that reflects its value. If you operate a coffee shop, your product ladder might look something like this:

Small coffee: $2.50

Medium coffee: $3.25

Large coffee: $4.00

That's it. This is a very basic product ladder. It's the same product, but we're offering different sizes. And therefore each rung on the ladder is worth a little more.

Now let's go one level deeper. You might have customers who are happy with a brewed coffee. And they can spend a little more money to get a bigger size. But perhaps they want to go fancier.

Instead of a brewed coffee, they want a cappuccino. So you add that to your ladder. A cappuccino is a premium beverage. So a small one is $3.75. More than the brewed coffee.

And then you offer a latte. And an espresso. And a flat white.

You also sell iced coffee, cold brew, macchiato, and cortado. The list goes on.

Now a customer can spend $2.50 or 5x that amount.

That's a product ladder in action. And we're just getting started.

CHAPTER 68

The 4 F's of the Product Ladder

There are 4 ways to build your product ladder. I call it my 4 F's. They are:

1. Flavors

2. Frills

3. Fillers

4. Functions

We'll look at each one and how to use it. Then I'll share a bunch of examples. I want to make sure you really understand this. If you get the product ladder right, you'll be able to sell one thing for $100, $1,000, $10,000, or a lot more.

And that means your customers can take even more action.

No tricks. No magic. Pure strategy.

I'll tell you about the 4 F's in order from the simplest to the most complex. For now I just want you to understand what they are. Afterwards we'll talk about how to implement them.

Okay friends, here are my 4 F's for building the product ladder.

CHAPTER 69

Flavors

The most basic way to add value in the product ladder is to change the flavor of the product. Of course, I'm not talking about the actual flavor, since that would only apply to food and drinks. I'm talking about keeping the product as it is, with a subtle change that provides the customer with a slightly different sensation.

Common flavor changes are size, packaging, materials, and colors.

If you're selling phone covers, maybe you offer the same one in 4 different colors. Two of them are standard colors at one price. And two of them are premium colors at a higher price.

If you sell flowers, you can sell a standard bouquet at one price. A premium bouquet with more flowers and colors at a higher price. And a luxury bouquet at the highest price.

These are all flavor changes because the product is essentially the same. But the customer is getting more perceived value at each point.

CHAPTER 70

Frills

A simple way to move products up the ladder is with frills. Little touches that give the product the appearance of being better. Whether or not the product is actually better is subjective. But at least you can make the case.

A frill is an enhancement to the product that's nice to have. But it's not necessary for the product to work.

The key to adding frills is to keep the core function of the product the same. Then spice it up however you can.

Take a hotel for example. I could give you a large suite, a better view, or a higher floor. These are all frills. And I can definitely justify a higher price. But the thing you're getting is still a hotel room.

There's a long list of frills you can add. Some strong areas to focus on are:

Convenience - can you give customers a more convenient way to use and enjoy your product?

Example: You could drive your car to the mechanic for tire maintenance. Or the mechanic can drive to you and service the vehicle in your driveway. This layer of convenience would increase the value and price.

Access - can you give people early access to something that isn't available to the general public?

Example: A concert can sell access to the sound check. Fans can watch the band prepare for the show ahead of time. This level of access would increase the value and price.

Status - can you allow customers to portray themselves to others as an amplified version of how they see themselves? If so, you've tapped into status.

Example: A club will set up a VIP area behind a velvet rope. The high rollers can hang out there. There's no difference between this area and the rest of the club. But the status bump would increase the value and price.

Comfort - Creature comforts go a long way. Make the experience a little more comfortable and people will pay up.

Example: Upgrade to a business class ticket on an airline for more legroom and a fully reclining seat. This extra comfort would increase the value and price.

Exclusivity - Give customers access to a certain type of thing for a certain period of time.

Example: You can buy sneakers for $125 or get this new pair of sneakers for $200. This exclusive offer would increase the value and price.

Priority - Let people get something before anyone else.

Example: You could sell tickets to your event beginning on a certain day. But customers can also pay extra for first dibs. This early entry would increase the value and price.

Peace of mind - Give the customer an insurance policy against the unexpected, so they can sleep well at night.

Example: Offer "A" is final sale. Offer "B" comes with a 90-day warranty. The products are identical in each offer. But the warranty would increase the value and price.

I'm sure there are even more frills that I haven't thought of. But this should get your brain brewing all the ways you can add frills to your product. And drive it up the product ladder.

CHAPTER 71

Fillers

Another way to stack up the product ladder is by adding fillers. These are complementary products that fill in the gaps which will naturally appear when the customer buys your product. And since they fill in the gaps, I call them "fillers".

For example, if I run a fitness center, my customers are signing up to use the fitness equipment in my gym. What are some other things they might need? How about a personal trainer to give clients guided fitness classes? Maybe a nutritionist to assist with their diet? Or maybe some workout clothing? These are all things that I can offer.

These aren't frills because they are actually different products from the main product I'm selling. Hypothetically, if I wasn't selling my main product, I could still sell the filler. Whereas frills are just enhancements to the main product. You can't sell them on their own.

To add fillers within your product ladder, ask yourself this question:

What new needs are being created by the needs I'm solving?

In the fitness center example, giving people access to a workout facility naturally makes them want to improve their workout regimen. And a personal trainer does this. To aid in weight loss, a nutritionist makes lots of sense. And going to the gym 3-4 times a week necessitates the right clothing. So selling clothes makes sense.

To decide which fillers to add, just listen and observe your customers. You'll quickly see what they're doing to fill the gaps on their own. Going back to the coffee shop example, you might notice that people are buying a coffee, then heading next door to buy a cookie or a donut. Why not add those to your menu?

Through listening and asking some questions, customers will tell you everything you need to know.

Of course, you shouldn't jump on every request a customer throws at you. Fillers should be added thoughtfully and strategically. Only when clear demand is presented to you.

CHAPTER 72

Function

The most extreme addition to your product ladder is a change in product function. This means you're fundamentally altering the thing your product does. In other words, you're adding a new product.

This usually happens when companies get into adjacent industries. It's last on the list because it's the hardest thing to do. Operationally speaking, you could be adding a lot of complexity to your business. And not only could that set you up for failure, it could also jeopardize the main thing you do because of the distraction.

If you are going to do it, here is a clear example:

I have a roofing company. It's an amazing business with a strong team and a steady flow of customers. A well-oiled machine.

But I'm also getting lots of requests to replace windows and doors.

Roofing does have some overlap with repairing windows and doors. The tradespeople who repair roofs might also repair windows and doors. And the homeowners who get their roofs repaired might also want their windows and doors repaired.

But that's likely where the overlap stops.

Things like suppliers, processes, project timelines, branding, marketing, and service guarantees would all be different. So you'd better ensure your main business is already thriving before exploring this new one.

Some people confuse "fillers" with "function". But there's a big difference between the two.

Fillers are things that solve a new need that opened up as a result of the main problem you solved. And for someone to buy the filler, they would have already bought the main thing.

Function is actually a whole new thing. It doesn't require someone to buy the first thing. They could just start with the new thing.

You are adding a different product to your mix. So why am I even including it here on the Product Ladder?

The reason I include it on the Product Ladder is because it's adjacent to the thing you already do. So there is some synergy. If you're selling boats and suddenly you want to open a zoo, I would say that's definitely not a function change on the Product Ladder.

You're just starting a whole different business.

But if you truly have a business firing on all cylinders, and customers are begging you for something new – I wouldn't ignore them.

CHAPTER 73

Product Ladder in Action

You run into product ladders everyday. You might not even notice it, but the best companies are built on them. Sturdy ladders. With rungs that keep on climbing.

It's why car companies have different models. It's why restaurants have menus. It's why software companies offer 5 different pricing plans.

When your customer buys into your unifying belief, and has faith that you can deliver, you need to be ready for them to take action. As much as they want.

Let's look at a clear example of a product ladder: a hotel.

Hotels range in price widely. You could stay at a hostel for $25 a night. Or a luxury resort for $5,000 a night. But here's what you need to remember. The person paying $50 and the person paying $5,000 are both getting the same thing: a place to sleep.

Surely that can't be the case, right? How could someone pay 200x more money and get the same thing? The reason is because of flavors, frills, fillers, and functions.

The 4 F's of a $25 room will be very different from the $5,000 version.

Let's look at both.

Example A: $50 Hotel

I walk into a dated room with a bed and a small window. The paint on the walls is chipping. Or at least, I think this room was painted at some point. There's a shared bathroom, but I'll try to hold it in for as long as I can. I don't want to go near that place. There's also a guy named Doug sharing the room with me. He was here when I walked in. He seems nice, but I'm going to keep my bag close anyhow.

Example B: $5,000 Hotel

I pull up to a beautiful building in the middle of a bustling downtown. A well-dressed man opens my car door and welcomes me by name. He says they've been expecting me and are delighted that I've arrived. I reach for my bag, but he insists I leave everything. He will handle it all. A lady appears beside me with a big smile and a lovely accent. She asks me to come with her and escorts me to my suite. Along the way she tells me that if I need anything at all, my butler Armando is just outside my door and can assist at a moment's notice. I walk into my suite and I'm struck by the sweeping views. The champagne is waiting and a soft tune plays on the grand piano. There are 3 balconies and the greatest fruit platter you could imagine.

———

Now you can see the difference between $50 and $5,000. Can you spot the 4 F's at work?

Let's review it together.

Flavors

Every single flavor between Examples A and B is different. And because the differences are so extreme, I actually wouldn't even think of them as flavor changes. They fall more into frills and fillers.

Let's explore why.

Frills

Lots of the differences fall into "frills". Think about the man carrying my bags or the woman escorting me to my suite. These are enhancements that aren't required for the product itself. I could easily carry my own bags or find my own way to the suite. But the perceived value is elevated with these touches.

You can probably imagine lots of other frills that would come with a $5,000 hotel room. Such as a much larger suite, express check-in, a plush duvet, high end art, a chauffeured limo from the airport, and so on.

There's a lot you could offer across status, convenience, exclusivity, priority, and the rest. All of these increase the value and the price.

Fillers

Things like the champagne, fruit platter, and butler are fillers. These things all compliment the main thing, which is the hotel.

Remember, these are fillers and not frills because they aren't just enhancements. Rather, they are separate items entirely. In this setting fillers are very important because they provide an "all-inclusive" experience. I don't need to worry about grabbing a snack or bringing my own alcohol. The hotel thought of that for me.

Functions

As crazy as it is to believe, the function of the $50 hotel and the $5,000 are the same. They both provide shelter and a place to sleep. Of course you could make the argument that other functions are being served in the $5,000 suite.

For example, the fruit platter is providing a meal. And a meal is different than shelter.

The reason I still put this under filler is because no one is going to this hotel specifically for a fruit platter. And the hotel probably doesn't specialize in selling fruit platters to the public. It's a specific filler for a specific product.

If the hotel decided to add a casino where people could come and gamble, that would certainly be a function change. But in the current example, the function doesn't change one bit.

CHAPTER 74

When to add Flavors, Frills, Fillers, and Functions

You should build on the 4 F's in the same order that I shared them here. That will keep things simple and allow you to max out the low hanging fruit before you move on to a tougher step.

Expanding the flavors of your product would be the first step. Then try adding frills to build on the value with minimal effort. Next you can add in fillers, which are more complex, but can also be very profitable. And last would be a new function. This is one that you might never need to do. But it's an option nevertheless.

Depending on your business, some of these things might make more sense than others.

If you're selling something very inexpensive, you're more likely to focus on flavors like size and quantity. For example, if your product is $20, consider selling a 3-pack for $50.

On the other hand, if you're selling something very expensive, you may focus on frills and fillers. Your $10,000 package could be elevated to $25,000 with more convenience, access, and related services.

And if you've completely topped out on what you can sell, a new function might be the key to your growth. Just be sure you're not lying to yourself. I've seen many businesses with so much opportunity for growth in their current business, that convince themselves to launch something new. Then you wind up with 2 mediocre offerings, when just one could be dramatically bigger.

———

Section 7: Recap

- Action is the money-making part of the Movement Formula. It's where people buy something from you, to fulfill the unifying belief and faith you have built.
- Drive action by focusing on the right type of content for your business:
    - For physical products, focus on benefits, usage, and value – then sell the product.
    - For services, provide content on service benefits, value, and DIY aspects – then sell the implementation.
    - For information offerings, create content around the 3 W's and go deep on narrow subjects – then sell the information.
- The Product Ladder lets customers take more action. You increase the value per customer and sell more stuff.
- There are 4 ways to build a product ladder: Flavors, Frills, Fillers, Functions.
- Add them in that order to keep things simple.

Bonus material:

I made a video that goes deeper on the product ladder. I explain how you can sell the same thing for $200 or $200,000, or a lot more. Understanding this really opened my eyes to the power of creating more value for your customers.

You can watch the video now at JonDavids.com/ProductLadder

Or snap the QR code below:

SECTION 8

Hacking the Axis

CHAPTER 75

Reality Check

Now you have all the key ingredients you'll need to achieve marketing superpowers.

Let's do a recap:

- You know how influence is built through my *Axis of Influence*

- You know how to develop an origin story with my *Origin-8 Framework*

- You know how to communicate your message through my *7 ground rules of copywriting* and the AIDA framework

- You know how to create a movement using my *Movement Formula*

- You know how to craft a unifying belief using my *5 Belief Builders*

- You know how to fuel faith through my *4 Faith Groups* and *10 Faith Drivers*

- You know how to maximize action through the *Product Ladder*

Now I'll finish off with a smack of reality. Get ready for a harsh truth. Because here it is:

This is going to be tougher than it sounds. For a while at least.

If you're a marketing executive at a big company with a budget to burn, get ready to ignite some flames. And if you're an entrepreneur or small business owner with no cash to waste, get ready to grind.

But I promise you the outcome is worth it. Marketing superpowers are worth every dollar and every minute they consume.

It's just not going to be a smooth ride.

You're going to encounter friction and obstacles. You're going to linger in Anonymity for what feels like forever. You're going to make content no one cares about. You're going to struggle to create an origin story that makes any sense. You're going to wonder why no one gives a crap about your movement. You're going to sputter, trying to come up with a piece of content that is even half decent.

And you're going to wonder if those Marketing Superpowers will ever show up. Or has your buddy JD just been lying to you this whole time?

I'm not. I promise. I know it works. Because I've been through it over and over again.

But since all of this is going to happen, I want to arm you with a few tactics now to keep you going. Not just that, but tactics you can use to improve along the way. So you're actually getting better over time. So that when you do make the crossover from Anonymity to the Influence, you'll be ready for it.

If you really want to see the results of everything I've discussed in this book, this last section will be critical.

Let's tackle it together.

CHAPTER 76

Tactics to Hack the Axis

I call this "Hacking the Axis" because that's what you'll be doing. Experimenting with different ways to advance your brand along the Axis of Influence. From the very beginning to the very end.

Here's a list of 11 effective ways you can hack the Axis. I'm sure there are ways I haven't even thought of. And by the time you read this book, I may have brewed up a bunch more.

Let's start with these:

1. Work on your storytelling

2. Focus on your hooks

3. Show your personality

4. Try different platforms

5. Try a different form of content

6. Piggyback the known with the unknown

7. Collaborate with others

8. Be different

9. Embrace the haters

10. Hit the reset button

11. Tweak your main character

Be sure to join my email list to keep up with new tactics that I'm sharing all the time. Subscribe for free at JonDavids.com.

Now we'll look at each one in more detail.

CHAPTER 77

Work on your storytelling

I'll assume that on day one, you are not a master storyteller. And that's okay. It took me a long time to learn the craft of storytelling. And I'm still getting better everyday.

The truth is, until you get decently good at this, it's difficult to break through.

I use the term "storytelling" loosely. I don't mean that all content will literally be telling stories. I'm referring to the idea that you need to keep people interested in what you're saying. And that usually involves some type of a story. It follows the AIDA framework.

That story could be 25 words or 2,500 words. It could be written or spoken. It could be about math or marriage or monkeys or military history. Whatever you're talking about, you need to make it interesting.

So if your reach is not growing, the first thing to look at is your storytelling. Is it sharp and easy to understand? Is it compelling? Is it gripping? Does it grab your audience by the collar and yank them in?

Your first attempts at making content will suck. It just won't be that good. It never is. You need to find your voice. Figure out how to tell your brand stories in a compelling way. Through the lens of your main character.

Improving your storytelling is the first thing you should work on and the thing you will never stop working on. Being in Anonymity is a serious luxury at this stage. Because your early work will be embarrassing. If it's not embarrassing, you're probably not trying hard enough. Or you're waiting too long to get content out into the wild.

So use your period of Anonymity wisely. Experiment, make mistakes, get better, fall on your face, take chances, and push boundaries.

This can take a while, but keep going. It's a saga, not a sprint.

CHAPTER 78

Focus on your hooks

Even if 95% of your storytelling is awesome, you might be missing the most important piece of all: the hook.

Your hook is the most important part because it's first. Your reader or viewer will make a split second decision based purely on your hook. If you don't hook them, it's over. Completely and utterly over. Pack it up, call it a day, nothing to see here.

Work and rework your hooks. Show them to friends and family. And ask one simple question: "Do these few words make you want to read more?"

If the answer is no, go back to the drawing board.

I've written hooks that didn't perform. And then by adding, cutting, or swapping just one word, they were read by 100,000 people. When your hook is on the line, sweat the details. You must capture attention at the very beginning or everything else you write is meaningless. Utterly worthless. Totally useless. It serves no purpose. Because it will never be seen.

Here's a perfect example in the power of the hook.

I wrote a story about a cab driver who became a billionaire. I posted this story to LinkedIn in September 2022.

Here's the hook I used: *In 1984, an immigrant landed in NYC with $50. Now he's making millions off gas stations and convenience stores.*

This story was read by 28,000 people. Not bad, right? I thought it was okay. But I also felt it could be better. So a few months later, I changed the hook and posted it again.

Here's hook #2: *Harry started as a broke cab driver and is now making millions with gas stations and convenience stores.*

This time the story was read by just 8,000 people. Yikes. Wrong direction.

So a few months later, I took a third swing. Here's hook #3: *I just heard about a cab driver who became a billionaire with one key insight.*

Jackpot. The third post was read by 64,000 people. That's 129% increase in readers. Plus I got tremendous engagement.

Think about that for a moment. All 3 of these posts were identical, except for the opening line. That's the power of a hook

CHAPTER 79

Show your personality

As your storytelling and copywriting improve, you may still not be breaking through. So let's talk about personality. Specifically, the personality coming through in your main character. If there's zero personality coming through, you're in trouble.

People love a good message, but they really love a good messenger. Who is the person behind this? That's also why the classic "brand" is resonating less with consumers today. Because they feel that no one is behind it. Old-school brands lack personality. They're stiff and dusty.

If I'm into a restaurant, I want to hear from the chef. If I'm into a sport, I want to hear from the athletes. If I'm into a movie, I want to hear from the actors. If I'm into a song, I want to hear from the artist.

The *who* is as important as the *what*. So if your content is not hitting a nerve, it could be missing personality.

Personality shines through in the way you speak, in the illustrations you paint, in the characters you introduce, in the references you drop.

For example, there's a guy I know on X (formerly Twitter) who always talks about how he loves the restaurant Chili's. This guy is a wealthy businessman, so it's kind of funny that he constantly tosses in the Chili's reference. It gives him personality. Makes him memorable.

There's an executive on LinkedIn who doles out smart financial advice. And she also throws in stories about her kids. They're a handful, they drive her crazy, but she loves them of course. The kids add personality to her content mix and make her relatable.

There's a podcast I listen to, where the host will reference his crazy neighbor. In fact, he references her so much that she's become a character on the show. Even though she's never actually been on the show. His sister adds some dimension to his personality.

The favorite restaurant, the wild kids, the crazy neighbor. These are just a few examples.

Maybe your main character is really into fishing, or photography, or watches, or aviation, or history, or knitting, or martial arts, or whatever. Bring it forward. Find the texture, swagger, mojo, humility. Find that relatable charm.

Make that personality pop.

CHAPTER 80

Try different platforms

Here's something you might not know. Before my content took off on LinkedIn, I tried posting very similar content to X, which was then called Twitter. And for some reason it didn't work. Zero engagement. Barely any impressions. No one cared.

I really don't know why.

My stories were strong, my copywriting was sharp and I was doing it consistently. But I was getting nowhere on X.

After months and months of trying, I was about to give up. I was wasting my time. Then I noticed something. A lot of people were posting content to X. But they didn't stop there. They posted the same content to LinkedIn. And they were doing this every day. Copy+paste from one platform to the other.

Sometimes the content would perform well on both platforms. Sometimes it would do well on just one and the other would flop.

It seemed strange, but it actually made sense as I thought about it.

People go to different platforms for different things. You might visit Instagram for celebrity photos, YouTube for cooking advice, TikTok for puppy videos, X for politics, and LinkedIn for career advice.

And someone else might visit Instagram for sports, YouTube for parenting, TikTok for travel, X for finance, and LinkedIn for restaurant industry news.

Everyone's media diet is different. And certain content works better on some platforms than others. I could go into endless detail on why and how your content might perform on each platform. But honestly, it's not worth the time. You're better off just experimenting to see what happens.

That's exactly what I did. That day, I began taking all my X content and posting it directly to LinkedIn. Boom. It blew up.

Even today, I'll post the exact same content to both LinkedIn and X. The same story will get 100,000 views on one platform and only 5,000 views on the other. Does one algorithm like me better than the other? I really don't know. But that's just the reality of making content.

If your content isn't attracting an audience on one platform, try another. Try them all. Platforms are like real estate. Location matters. Take the same content and move it over somewhere else.

You just might be surprised by what a difference this makes.

CHAPTER 81

Try a different form of content

Before you started making content, you probably put some thought into the form of that content. You either chose written content like a blog, audio content like a podcast, visual content like a Pinterest board, or video content like YouTube videos.

If one isn't working for you, I encourage you to try the others. It's possible that the form you're using isn't the best fit for the market you're trying to reach. And it might not be the optimal way for you to tell the story. There could also be a mismatch between the form and platform. For example, my video content does quite well on YouTube. But when I try to post those same videos to LinkedIn, they don't perform quite as well.

I've noticed other people don't have this problem. Some people post videos to LinkedIn and they get loads of exposure. I just don't see those same results. Now, I could sit around and wonder why this is. But that's not worth my time. I want to deal with reality on reality's terms. I want to move forward and get things done. Not wish, wonder, and worry. So I stick with what works for me.

Certain platforms favor different content forms for different users.

If content form A isn't working, try B, C, or D. Then try combining those forms with different platforms. Long form video on X, audio posts on X, Text videos on TikTok, short form videos on TikTok, written posts on LinkedIn, short form videos on LinkedIn. The list goes on.

Don't get stuck on one form. A better one could be a click away.

CHAPTER 82

Piggyback the known with the unknown

People are naturally more attracted to things they know versus things they don't know. The food I know, the people I know, the movies I know, the songs I know, the places I know, the books I know, and so on.

One thing that makes social media so addictive is that it's all about you. The platforms learn who and what you're into. And they serve up just those things. You can spend hours scrolling and you never seem to get bored. Why is that?

Because the platform is only showing *you* what you want to see.

And we can leverage that principle in our content. Through the power of association, we can piggyback the unknown on top of the known.

For example, if you're writing a piece targeting the audience in a certain city, start with a reference to a local landmark. Something like this:

I was at Bill's Diner last night. I had the Reuben Sandwich with a side of Loaded Fries. It was so good. If you've been to Bill's, you know what I'm talking about.

People in the city who know Bill's Diner are going to pay attention. You have them hooked. If it's written content, you could have a photo of Bill's Diner beside the post. If it's video content, your thumbnail and opening screen could be a visual of Bill's Diner. If it's a podcast, the title could be "The Best Thing To Eat at Bill's Diner."

The KLT that's already associated with Bill's Diner – and presumably Bill, the main character of the diner – will naturally rub off on you.

Now you can piggyback off Bill's Diner to weave into the thing you want to talk about. You can do the same thing with other known things:

- Celebrities

- Movies

- Books

- Institutions

- Politicians

- News events

- Recipes

- Memes

- Viral videos

- Online trends

The list is endless. The key is to identify something people are already interested in and find a way to latch your thing onto that thing. The more you do this, the better you'll get. It's really just a matter of reps.

So get creative. And get your piggyback on.

CHAPTER 83

Collaborate with others

This one takes more leg work but it's well worth it. If you can build relationships with others in your space and start making content together, you can fast-track your growth big time.

The problem here is that most people aim way too high, way too soon. They go for the most famous, most successful, most visible person in their category. The person who gets countless requests every day. This is not what you should do. First off, it's unlikely that you'll get anywhere with this approach. And if you're really early in your journey, you probably aren't ready for the main stage. Remember, you must make mistakes in the dark so you can shine in the light.

A better strategy is to approach someone who is 1 or 2 steps ahead of you. Just doing a little better. Maybe they started a few months earlier or they've just happened to hit on something that resonated quicker. So they're a bit further along. These people need more help. They'll be more receptive to a collaboration. And you may be able to legitimately help them with something they haven't caught onto yet.

To collaborate, you can interview them, profile them, play a game with them, or take them to lunch and share the experience with your audience. This is very similar to the piggyback approach I discussed earlier. But instead of just talking about someone else, you're collaborating with them to make the content.

The right combination can be a speedpass for both of you.

CHAPTER 84

Be different

This one sounds obvious. And that's because it is. It's also the most common reason that brands and characters never break out. Because they blend into a sea of sameness. They see one brand doing something successfully, and they figure "I'll do the same thing."

The problem is that now you're playing for sloppy seconds. Why would I want imitation Coke when I can get the real thing? The original? That's what I want. Not some weird clone that's 72% as good.

But it doesn't stop there. You're also now competing with a bunch of other people who had the same idea. They saw someone hit on a winning formula and now they're doing it too. So you're not just competing with the real thing, you're competing against a whole bunch of imitators.

You wind up looking played out. A cheap knockoff that's not ready for prime time. Because no one wants your reheated leftovers.

What's the solution?

I already told you. Be different.

Different style, different messaging, different twist, different look, different vibe, different everything. When one group is being super-served, there are others who aren't being served at all. So look around. Look deeper. Around the edges.

In the cooking space, you see polished videos of people cooking healthy food from scratch. You also see raw, offbeat videos of people cooking the most absurd things, that no one would ever possibly think of eating. These are 2 totally different approaches to food. Both serve an audience of people who want food content.

It's the same. But totally different.

CHAPTER 85

Embrace the Haters

In chapter 2, I told you about "anti-KLT". That's when people know you, but they don't like you, and they definitely don't trust you. Plus they scream it from the rooftops. These people are your loudest critics. Your detractors. Giving you a side-eye from across the room.

And if you're lucky enough to have them, it means you're making a dent in the culture. We see this all over society. In medicine, sports, business, politics, law, and beyond. Anyone with a megaphone who does something that a certain group of people don't agree with, gets criticized. And that criticism cranks up the volume.

And as long as you're acting responsibly and legally, this is a smart growth tactic. But how do you actually do it?

In chapter 34, I told you how to create polarization. And now I'll share an advanced tactic. I call this the "common enemy". This is where you rally your believers by throwing stones at an "enemy" that gets under their skin. It's called a "common enemy" because these are big cultural representations.

For example:

- The '9-5' grind

- Traffic

- Lawyers

- Billionaires

- Government

- The 'elite'

- The 'boss'

- Cancer/illness

- Sugar

- The 'old' way

- The 'big' guys

We see politicians doing this all the time. Throwing shade at the "establishment" or cherry-picking their opponents policies and lambasting them. Because they can get a rise out of their supporters by inflaming them.

It's not hard to hate on common enemies. And it's actually socially acceptable to do so, especially within your tribe.

It's also okay if the common enemy is vague or inanimate. I'm not even sure what some of these are. What people refer to as 'elite' can vary widely. Things like 'the old way' and 'the new way' are completely open to interpretation. That's helpful because listeners will interpret on a personal level.

You can assign labels that benefit you and rally others over to the cause.

Let the haters make noise. And watch your loyalists jump into action.

CHAPTER 86

Hit the reset button

A time will come when you'll need to throw in the towel. Not forever. Just for a minute or two.

Here's what I've found on various media channels. If enough time has passed and you're really not getting anywhere, the best move can actually be to start all over again. Maybe your feeds have gone rusty. Or the algorithms just don't like you.

And if this is the case, it's time to start fresh.

To be fair, you're not actually starting from scratch. Because as a content creator, you will be 10, 20, or 30 times better than you were before. Plus you have a content library that you can re-use. You're just whipping up a new profile to restart the engine.

It sounds silly. But I've seen this happen for myself. Influicity took over management of a client's TikTok feed a year ago. We tried for months and months to jack up engagement. Different types of content and creative executions. Proven formulas that have worked on dozens of other channels.

But we weren't getting anywhere.

So we made a bold move. We asked the client if we could just start a new channel. They were hesitant of course. Because of all the work they had put into the current channel. But what were they really going to lose by starting again?

Did they have loyal followers? No.

Did they have excellent engagement? No.

Was their content being indexed highly on the platform? No.

All they had was a channel with a history of mediocre performance.

After a few conversations, they agreed. And we went ahead with our plan. We didn't delete the old channel, we just stopped posting on it. We registered a new username – a spin on the brand name – and started over.

From the very first post on the new channel, we saw a clear improvement. And 12 weeks later, we had the same number of followers on the new channel, as we did on the old channel. Plus the engagement on the new channel was much higher.

Fast forward 12 months, and we were at 4x the number of followers. More importantly, the engagement on each one of our posts was miles ahead of where they had been previously. And the feed looked better than ever.

I don't suggest taking this step lightly or rushing to it. But if you really have nothing to show after a long time, and you've gotten much better along the way, you may want to shake the Etch-A-Sketch and start fresh.

After all, you don't have much to lose.

CHAPTER 87

Tweak your main character

You've probably put a lot of effort into deciding on the main character. It might be you. Or your boss. Or your co-founder. Or some pretty face you've hired. And even though you felt it was a good choice, you're not the one who gets to decide. Your target customer is.

If you've given it a good amount of time and customers just aren't connecting, you may need to rethink the main character.

I'm not saying you should jump to replace them right away. You should try all the other hacks before this one. Work on the storytelling, focus on the hooks, evaluate the platforms, and so on.

Go back to the drawing board, tweak what you can, and try again.

And if all that fails, do what needs to be done. Switch up your main character. Easier said than done, of course. It's not pleasant to tell a person they don't have it. Whatever "it" is. But we're not here to be nice. We are here to build marketing superpowers. And the main character is a must.

If you've picked the wrong main character, fire them. It's not personal, it's just business.

CHAPTER 88

You will need to change along the way

And now for the realest reality check of them all. You will absolutely, positively need to change your approach as you scale. No matter what.

The stuff that got you from 0 - 1,000 followers might not get you to 10,000 followers. And what got you to 10,000 definitely won't get you to 1,000,000. This means that at one point or another, you will need to hack the axis.

Why do we need to change our strategies as we move up? There are lots of reasons: copycats, audience fatigue, culture shifts, and platform changes to name a few. But there are two really important reasons to understand:

1. Staying relevant

As you grow, you will need to reinvent yourself if you want people to keep caring. It's only natural for a brand to morph in an ever-changing culture. That's how you maintain interest from current fans and attract new ones.

People love "new". We often associate new with better. It may not be, but that's what people assume. Don't fight it – leverage it.

Observe how customers are shifting around you. What do they care about? Where do they hang out? What shows do they watch? What bugs them? What delights them?

Staying on the pulse will keep you relevant.

2. Finding new audience

A flourishing fish eventually outgrows its pond. With success, that will happen to your brand too. Your market will stop growing because you've capped out on that particular segment. And that's not a bad thing. It just means you need to widen your thinking.

I know a guy who built a big audience discussing personal finance. He owned a wealth management company and used his personal finance content to grow the business. He did extremely well with this. Then he started to launch new businesses and expanded his content outwards. He discussed politics, sports, cars, and more.

Of course, these topics have nothing to do with each other. And they're a world away from personal finance. But this particular influencer had already conquered that first category. And a second, and a third. He went from an audience of 50,000 to 300,000 to 1 million, to 3 million and beyond. He was finding new audiences and expanding his market opportunities.

This may be levels ahead of where you are today. That's okay. You'll get there. And when you do, you'll need to make changes in order to hack the axis.

———————

Section 8: Recap

- You can hack the Axis to drive your growth further, faster
- Here are my 11 tips to hack the Axis:
    1. Work on Your Storytelling
    2. Focus on Your Hooks
    3. Show Your Personality
    4. Try Different Platforms
    5. Try a Different Form of Content
    6. Piggyback the Known with the Unknown
    7. Collaborate with Others
    8. Be Different
    9. Embrace the Haters
    10. Hit the Reset Button
    11. Tweak your main character
- No matter what, you'll need to change along the way
- Adapt strategies as the audience and platform dynamics evolve
- Stay current and relevant with new audiences to sustain growth

Bonus material:

I created a checklist on all the ways you can hack the axis. Grab a copy and scan it whenever you need some inspiration on hitting the gas.

Get it now at JonDavids.com/MarketingSuperpowers.

Or snap the QR code below:

CLOSING

CHAPTER 89

Somewhere in Mexico

January 4, 2023

My feet are sweating. I haven't worn shoes in 4 days. Who needs shoes on a velvety beach?

My 4-year old Ryley is building a sand castle. My 2-year-old Mikki is napping by the pool. My wife Alana is reading a book while I fiddle with my phone. Trying to capture that perfect angle for a photo of this turquoise Cancun view.

My thumb is moving in for the snap. Just then, a notification pops up over the button. I tap it by mistake.

Damn it. Now I have to reset the frame.

It's a LinkedIn notification. I'm curious, so I swipe open the app. One new message waiting.

It's the CEO of a 170-person textile company. Let's call him Lewis.

Lewis has been following me online for months. He reads my posts. Gets my weekly newsletter. Listens to my podcast. He's even been to a couple Influicity webinars. Lewis says he appreciates all my insights around digital marketing. He's learned so much. And he wants to set up a meeting next week to see how we can work together.

That meeting turned into a $400,000 contract for Influicity.

But that's not the point. Why did Lewis send me that message in the first place? By now you should know.

Because I created a unifying belief. And I backed it up with faith. So Lewis took action.

I provided so much value that it only made sense for him to make a move. I'm the main character in the story of Influicity. My brand means something. Lewis trusts it. Just like so many others.

My movement is about the power of building a customer community. Turning your brand into a movement. Making it so good that it's impossible to ignore.

This is what Influicity does for so many clients.

And that's why, while lying on a breezy beach and building castles in the sand, my movement continues.

Because marketing is my superpower.

And it really does feel like magic.

———

KEEP GOING

I've given you the formulas to win. Now it's up to you to put them to work. So here's what I want you to do next.

Download my free worksheets and guides at JonDavids.com/MarketingSuperpowers

Learn from my daily content across social media:

- in linkedin.com/in/jondavids
- ▶ youtube.com/@jondavids
- ◎ instagram.com/jon_davids
- ♪ tiktok.com/@jon_davids
- 𝕏 x.com/realjondavids

And tune into my podcast every week. You can find it now at JonDavids.com/Podcast

Book Jon Davids to speak at your event

Contact us at JonDavids.com/speaking

Marketing Superpowers Pro
The Complete Training System

If you want to go even deeper into the material of this book, we've developed a complete training system. It includes everything in this book plus our advanced curriculum.

Get it at MarketingSuperpowersPro.com

Thank you to my team

influicity

I want to extend a heartfelt thanks to my incredible
team at Influicity. To all my colleagues, past and
present — I couldn't do any of this without you!
Can't wait to see what we do next.

Printed in the USA
CPSIA information can be obtained
at www.ICGtesting.com
LVHW020959210624
783648LV00011B/675

9 781738 315208